LAPTOPRADIO LA RADIO SIAMO NOI

HEAD — Genève and Link Editions, 2019

I0422400

CONTENT

INTRODUCTION

Jonathan Frigeri, Ceel Mogami de Haas and Laurent Schmid

"Radio Alice retransmits: some music, news, gardens in bloom, a torrent of words, inventions, discoveries, recipes, horoscopes, magic potion, love, war bulletins, photographs, messages, massages, lies."
— Radio Alice

LAURENT SCHMID: LapTopRadio started as an open project some years ago in Geneva. This collaboration between some friends at HEAD's Work.Master program and people interested in doing experimental internet radio picked up threads of different formulations of doing radio today in a postmedia context. First, there was a desire to share experiences between artists, sound artists, musicians, poets, activists... and the public. And then, by questioning the media condition, discovering that by using the internet, a structure built for defense reasons, we redid in a way what was after Friedrich Kittler, the origin of radio broadcasts or even the whole entertainment industry: "The entertainment industry is, in any conceivable sense of the word, an abuse of army equipment." *Grammophon Film Typewriter*, dt: Berlin: Brinkmann & Bose, 1986, 149

We became aware that Radio Alice directly did this in 1976, their program was broadcast on an old army transmitter from Bologna. By going into the matter, we delved deeper into these media-related questions and decided to start research with a series of events and expositions. Our focus on the different possibilities of 'postmedia' practice drew upon Guattari's concept of social and media assemblages which unleash new forms of collective expression and experience.

We tried to question and to understand the actual parameters for what he claimed in his later texts, e.g. in "Pour une éthique des médias" in *le Monde* of Nov. 6. 1991 in which Guattari expressed his hope to switch from consensual mass-media to forms of dissensual post-media, mainly based on what he observed in terms of technological development, on a redefinition of the relation between consumers and producers and also on the institution of new social practices. We thus aimed to integrate technological questions and to relate them to intimacy, public and private sphere in spatiotemporal reasoning radio-territories, common spacing. And even to radio-magic, phantasmic radio, ether, non-visual and non-haptic space. An exhibition with talks, discussions, concerts, performances, screenings and a learn-in was a key early event for our research.

CEEL MOGAMI DE HAAS: What is at the heart of LapTopRadio is, *from my point of view,* experimentation and détournement (in the situationist understanding of rerouting) of sociotechnological interactions. As such we are consciously dealing with 'post-internet' or 'post-digital' paradigms while remaining within a 'post-media' practice "of collective-individual reappropriation and an interactive use of machines of information, communication, intelligence, art and culture" from Felix Guattari, unpublished text of October 1990, published in the journal Chimères, n.28, spring-summer 1996. I am stressing the fact that it is my point of view for I believe that there are a multitude of opinions based on the variety of experiences LapTopRadio has conducted and allowed. This diversity is essential, and it wouldn't be fair to expose my sole opinion as something primordial. We could say that LapTopRadio is a single event of the molecular revolution Guattari wrote about.

"Yes, I believe that there is a multiple people, a people of mutants, a people of potentialities that appears and disappears, that is embodied in social, literary, and musical events…. I think that we're in a period of productivity, proliferation, creation, utterly fabulous revolutions from the viewpoint of this emergence of a people. That's molecular revolution: it isn't a slogan or a program, it's something that I feel, that I live…". from Felix Guattari, *Molecular Revolution* In Brazil, 2007 cit. after Suely Rolnik

LS: Yes, we were especially attracted by Guattari's specific approach to the radio and the fact that he was mainly interested in its form and social organization. It was less a critique of the media's application by the power, but he understood a free radio practice as a functional and pragmatic tool for examining its role as a key for a struggle over the contemporary production of consensual subjectivity. And this is a point I was and still am very interested in, since our current political, economic and cultural situation has manifestly not improved in the meantime. So we took up his idea of what I would call "deterritorialized micro radios" as a possibility of "miniaturization of forms of expression," which

are making possible new forms of sensibility and sociability by rather creating connections between emerging subjectivities than pointing to a big new idea or concept.

JONATHAN FRIGERI: It's why a spontaneous and fresh attitude took over on most projects we made. This approach, which also came from Radio Alice's attitude where everything was possible and open, like creating the whole day's radio schedule the same morning in front of coffee and cigarettes. This movement left an interesting openness to surprises and magical errors like in every day (real) life. Improvisation has often been the under the breath of the LTR's collective. Of course, improvisation asks to be aware of an important quantity of information, understanding, analyzing and reacting as Fred Frith explains in his text:

"Being able to do what you want to do; being alert to, and present in, the moment; awareness of your physical and social environment; the ability to listen alertly and in detail and instantly to translate what you hear into a possibility or an opportunity; and the ability to change your course of action without hesitation if the situation demands

LaRadioSiamoNoi: *Extended Nervous Systems and White Rabbits* exhibition view with neon work by Maurizio Nannucci

CMH: I remember that at one point, LapTopRadio adopted Radio Alice's motto that clearly illustrates what Laurent is saying about 'emerging subjectivities' versus 'big new ideas':

"Radio Alice retransmits: some music, news, gardens in bloom, a torrent of words, inventions, discoveries, recipes, horoscopes, magic potion, love, war bulletins, photographs, messages, massages, lies". This watchword also highlights the willpower to abolish hierarchies so that everyone and everything is allowed to participate.

Participation is also a key notion in our projects; improvised—leading sometimes to these 'magical errors' Jonathan is referring to—direct, open, sometimes conflictual, mostly harmonious, participation is present at all stages of our project: from the design of the open-source software to the collective program.

LS: There is also another important point in this short motto: like optical media, recorded sound is often understood as a central activity to the making of history—mainly through the fact that sounds and images become audible or visible as mediated events. The past in these events is an imagined place where linear concepts of history become questionable, where images and text are subject to a blending of fact and fiction. Walter Benjamin's idea that the past and the present create a flickering or erratically appearing constellation, at least in the dialectic sense, was an important influence; it gave us the possibility to incorporate a nonlinear and fragmented narrative in order to produce a situation with modes of representation that create relationships to what is past while simultaneously appropriating the present. The sounds themselves, the texts were not understood as a substance, but as a relationship touching specific points of views on relations of power, and the roles of the individual and the group in the context of our activities.

We were, and still are, dealing with different forms of interest in parallel; poetry, music, sound experiments, but also social and political theory, economic structures and media-related issues. By the dialectical use of all these combinations, the different components of this system are shaped and sharpened and become not only tools to understanding the other components and our activity itself but also—as an experimental system—work-units and process-units to investigate where and how this artistic experimental constellation and social reality come in contact with one another.

Our radio projects are experimental systems on two levels, created in a processual way within a given and predefined condition and on the other hand it has its epistemic side for the listener although it shows the

Wonderlust, at Fabbrica Rosa with Kenneth Goldsmith, Ingeborg Lüscher and Una Szeemann

sporadic, unpredictable, and irregular nature of the used element's occurrence. They are embedded in time, and can be understood as different bundles with their own temporality, evolving and expanding while interacting with neighboring systems.

CMH: This rhizomatic structure you're talking about is what you start to see more accurately once you step away from it. The website's archive, for example offers a vast and complex genealogy with branches growing everywhere. And it becomes very challenging, if not aberrant, to try and define this heterogeneous multitude. The often performative quality of the broadcasts adds to the difficulty of recollection. These broadcasts are anchored in a practice—visual arts for LapTopRadio is a project that originates first within an art school—that is so polymorphous that it almost seems to me that we conceived a radio that in fact resists radio.

JF: I would call it "organic structure" or "delirium display".
The idea that Laurent announces: different forms of interest in parallel.　　　　　These actions and reactions to a flow of things, related and unrelated to each other. I find that some principles of the technique of "stream of consciousness" A stream of consciousness is a narrative mode or device that depicts the multitudinous thoughts and feelings which pass through the mind. have always been, in a way or another, present in the creative process of LapTopRadio projects. The multi subjective experience mixed together became collective reality, the destruction of the strict linear time narration approach to the irrational/rational thoughts of every

character participating. We cannot really call it an interior monologue, as for the literary movement, due to its collective nature. It's more a combined cut-up. You control what you put in, but you don't fully control what comes out.

It's like every morning when you wake up.

LS: Our idea was to create a framework, which encourages and boosts all these possible paths. We were very much interested in open structures, but it was also necessary to create specific environments that made possible all these itinerant flows. First of all we started with a multi-layer project at LiveInYourHead, Geneva, an art space related to HEAD-Geneva, directed by Yann Chateigné: "*L aRadi o Siamo Noi*— Extended Nervous Systems and White Rabbits" was at the same time an exhibition, a series of talks and screenings, a pedagogical project with teach-ins and discussions, concerts and broadcasts. The exhibition was conceived and realized with the great help of Mathieu Copeland, besides a radio-like, invisible part, neon-works by Stefan Bruggemann, Cerith Wyn Evans and Alan Vega around a central piece by Maurizio Nannucci which we had the chance to produce anew for the exhibition. On the ceiling, we had around forty FM emitters with on each a sound related to the history of free radios in Italy. These different "programs" could be heard on headphones under each emitter in the exhibition space. A special part of the exhibition at LiveInYourHead, was created by a group led by Willem van Weelden from DOGtime IDUM at Gerrit Rietveld Academie, Amsterdam: "The Kafka Machine: a Three Hour Testament".

The project aimed to provide a platform for an exchange on self-organized media, media-activism, radio-magic and related artistic practices during and around the 1970s in Italy, and a reflection on the impact and the aftermath of this set of innovative concepts today.

We were interested in the possibilities for integrating and harnessing the good energy of these movements and projects and raised the question which ideas, which concepts are still worth transferring into the actual discourse. What is the role of self-organization and self-teaching in the field of free radio making and related cultural practices in a very different, but still difficult political and cultural context? What does it mean in a situation in which culture has become one of the most prestigious forms of consumption, and social activities can be translated into financial figures, where contacts, or "Friendships" suddenly become a value that can be sold?

Although the situation has deeply changed since the seventies, and the boundaries between consumption, information, cognition and communication have been even more blurred, we thought that there are reasons to look back at this scene, which showed a high level of critical consciousness with explicit and well articulated discourses. The structures collapsed in the meantime and also the weakness of some of these projects and concepts emerge nowadays, but we also observe that the specific situation led to a unique interlacing of design, media, arts and critical culture.   Central questions were: Can we escape the recuperation of experimental strategies from that period, but voided of any contestatory dimension and with the implicit resurgence of a mode of signification, a sympathy for "progressive" form without critical stakes? How can one ensure that the symptoms of this disengagement are recognized? What are possible counter-models? The events showed a wide variety of artists, writers, radio-activists, musicians and self-publishers. Speakers and participants included Lars Bang Larsen, Francesco Bernardelli

and Fabrizio Basso, Federico Campagna and Richard John Jones, Alfredo Cramerotti, Federica Martini, Vincent de Roguin, RadioArteMobile, Teatrino Elettrico, Sea Urchin and Willem van Weelden.

"*Wonderlust*—Inspiring adventures, explosive magic, free spirits, ludic interventions, and pataphysical solutions" was an itinerant project between Geneva and the Ticino we spent together with Kenneth Goldsmith and Mathieu Copeland and guests for ten days during the summer. The main idea was to bring together artists, curators, writers and motivated people form our LapTopRadio group, sharing fields of research, the reflections and questions they were working on in an atmosphere of trust. We met Paolo Coteni, Samuel Gross, Franco Lafranca, Quinn Latimer,

Live broadcast with Pacôme Thiellement. HFAD-Geneva

Ingeborg Lüscher, Jonas Olsson, Una Szeemann and Bohdan Stehlik—they organized a fantastic program in Ticino!—and Joël Vacheron.

The thematic framework was defined by their individual proposals and the resulting discussions in the group and also by the geographical and historical context. We aimed to make possible surprising encounters and exchanges, discussions in an open, free and stimulating structure, in a motivating context. It was an attempt to explore the possibilities of the critical and esthetical potential of LapTopRadio, its notion of place and corporeality. Wonderlust wanted to provide a rich, well-supported environment for organic and unforeseeable events to occur, for pooling knowledge, developing forms of attention but also for sharing uncertainties and exploring instabilities. A project of common learning and unlearning.   Practices included walks and visits, common activities and workshops, lectures, filmscreenings as well as dinner discussions—and daily broadcasts on LapTopRadio.org.

One other project which is worth being mentioned is a totally hybrid one; it shows quite accurately how projects evolved and the way we usually proceeded. Pedro Reyes was invited to show his project "Sanatorium" at dOCUMENTA (13) and he asked us at HEAD—Geneva if a group of students wanted to participate as what he called "therapists". Sanatorium was a transient clinic-like structure that provided short, unexpected treatments mixing art and psychology. Pedro had already shown the project balancing reality and parody in New York at the Guggenheim Museum's Stillspotting NYC. Because we were in contact and some of the therapists were members of the LapTopRadio collective at that time, we discussed the possibility of integrating it. Finally, there were some broadcasts realized, but in parallel a more important branch was developed by LapTopRadio member Andrea Marioni. Marioni was at dOCUMENTA (13) for the whole period, and he was also part of Dora Garcia's team and tried to derive benefit from all the artists and persons coming together in Kassel during the summer of 2012. So he started a series of broadcasts he called "back in '12" with various projects, ranging from transmissions of talks and performances to weird radio dramas and musical comedies, and also discussions like a "breakfast with Bifo". A transcript of a part of it can be found in this publication.

Some of the most important projects of LapTopRadio were:

LA RADIO SIAMO NOI
06.04.—26.05. 2012

Exhibition curated by Mathieu Copeland, Samuel Gross, Ceel Mogami de Haas and Laurent Schmid. Concerts were organized by Jonathan Zonoff Frigeri; the whole program was conceived by the LapTopRadio team with the help of Francesco Bernardelli, Federico Campagna and Richard John Jones, Alfredo Cramerotti, Lars Bang Larsen, Federica Martini, Vincent de Roguin, Sea Urchin, Willem van Weelden and a group of students of DOGtime, Gerrit Rietvelt

Academie, Amsterdam. A print on demand publication, designed by B&R, Noah Bonsma and Dimitri Reist was published for this occasion.

"DON'T WAIT FOR THINGS TO HAPPEN" 28.08.—06.09. 2012

with Eternal Tour at SESC-SP in São Paulo, curated by Donatella Bernardi. http://www.eternaltour.org/SP/120828_program_ENG.pdf

"WONDERLUST"

29.07.—06.08. 2013

Days in Geneva with Kenneth Goldsmith, Mathieu Copeland, Paolo Coteni, Samuel Gross, Quinn Latimer and Joël Vacheron. Ghost Tour in the Ticino with Kenneth Goldsmith, Ingeborg Lüscher, Una Szeemann and Bohdan Stehlik, Hetty Regantini, Franco Lafranca. Important moments: common dinners and dinner-discussions, screenings, mini-concerts in the evening.

Tactics: Consensus, Cooking, Listening, Magic, Music, Movement, Play, Reading, Walks, but also Dissensus, Sampling, Plundering, Cheating.

Keywords: Transversality, Cooperative Activity, Ritual, Performance, Poetry, Direct Action, Visits and Encounters, Collectivity, Potlach, Utopia, Anarchism.

"RADIO SANATORIUM, BACK IN '12" AND "BLITZKRUG" IN KASSEL, DURING DOCUMENTA (13)   09.06.—16.09. 2012

Broadcasts realized in the context of Pedro Reyes' project Sanatorium, and some events of the Maybe Education program done by members of LapTopRadio in parallel to dOCUMENTA (13) at different locations in Kassel.   With: Franco Bifo Berardi, Dora Garcia, Federico Campagna, Marcos Lutyens, Raimundas Malasauskas, Pedro Reyes, Charles Samons, Jan Mech, Pacôme Thiellement.

"FIGHT THE POWER", AT CORNER COLLEGE, ZÜRICH   05.11.2012

Fight the Power took place within the project This Machine Kills Fascists, inspired by Woodie Guthrie guitar inscription and dealing with protest songs in the widest meaning. The subject of the evening could be summarized as an attempt to analyze the geopolitics and dialectics of protest songs. That is for the theoretical part; pragmatically the broadcast consisted of a collective live atopic sound performance. A number of invited artists, writers, activist and musicians remotely contributed in real time.

Following projects include:

"Radio Tramontana", a series of projects the LapTopRadio group realized in the context of Viavai—contrabbando culturale svizzera-Lombardia by Pro Helvetia during autumn, winter spring 2014/15 in the region between the Ticino and northern Italy. (http://radiotramontana.cc.)

Broadcasts at Istitute Svizzero ISR in Milan and Maloya in November 2014, "Il problema della sicurezza", and ISR Rome "DIG" June 2015, or "Orgon Lunch (pausa pranzo lunga)" at museo MA★GA, Gallarate.

"Freundeskreise—Circoli degli amici", at Kunstmuseum Luzern in the context of the exhibition Sviluppo—Parallelo during November 2015 to January 2016 with several broadcasts in the Kunstmuseum.

Most programs were also streamed by RAM, www.radioartemobile.it and some were broadcast on FM by CoLaboRadio/senderberlin.org, Radio Campus Brussels and Radio Gwendalyn, Chiasso.

ITALIAN SHORTCUTS
Federica Martini

"Comrades, men and women. A friend of mine died today. He died because for some time he had given up on life, and this is what I would like to speak to you about. About life, not death... I am here today to speak to you about a personal problem of mine. There's talk, a buzzing in the hall. Yes, certainly. I am addressing this gathering in the form of an inquiry, and so I'll get right to the point (...): is it legitimate for an old comrade like myself to fall in love?" https://www.youtube.com/ watch?v=KsNBp68HkX0 (last accessed July 4, 2014).

So begins the speech that director Ettore Scola assigns to Mario, a member of parliament played by Vittorio Gassman in the movie *La terrazza* (1980). The context is a hypothetical 15th conference of the Italian Communist Party. Mario's confession, in the form of a desire, inserts a personal note into the party's proceedings and disrupts the institutional agenda.

Scola shot *La terrazza* during a seven-year period, between 1977 and 1984, a time lapse that, according to Umberto Eco, was characterized "by the discovery or rediscovery of the private realm, of needs, of the freedom of impulses." Umberto Eco, *Sette anni di desiderio*, Milan, Bompiani, 2006, p. 68. Back then, claims were made for the value of the present and the immediate state of permanent happiness. To this regard, Primo Moroni and Nanni Balestrini wrote that the year 1977 "represents a critique of every psychological investment in the future, and the claim for an immanence without residue, a living in the present that leaves no room for ideologies or expectations." Piero Moroni, Nanni Balestrini, *L'orda d'oro* (1968–1977. La grande ondata rivoluzionaria e creativa, politica ed esistenziale), Milano, Feltrinelli, 1997 There is undoubtedly something paradoxical when speaking about the future of a movement—the 'Seventy-seven creative wing'—that rejected the future as a cultural idea. In February 1977, when Umberto Eco reviewed the A/traverso collective's book titled *Alice è il diavolo—Sulla strada di Majakovskij: testi per una pratica di comunicazione sovversiva* (Alice is the devil—On the road to Mayakovsky: texts towards a practice of subversive communication), he imagined precisely this paradox, the future alternate history of the reader who discovers the publication *Alice is the devil* thirty years later, in 2007. A reader who, Eco writes, "would not see unemployed seasonal workers, hippies in station waiting rooms, naked bodies seeking some new contact" and who "if anything, would have the impression that a new 'cultural' group was speaking about these things, and inventing new channels and styles to do so." Umberto Eco, *Sette anni di desiderio*, op. cit. Unlike what Eco has proposed, the A/traverso collective's intention was not to speak of counterculture but to "produce texts in the street, to wildly celebrate life's transformations, to transform the color of cities and the language of all relationships, to make capitalistic servitude intolerable." Bifo, "Sulla strada per Majakovskij." *In A/traverso, giugno 1976, quoted in Claudia Salaris, Il movimento del Settantasette, immagini e scritture dell'ala creativa, Udine: AAA, 1997, p. 71.*

According to Majakovskij, the goal was "to make poetry and not the extraordinary." Ibidem. This desire to "spectacularly" abolish the distinction between art and life led the A/traverso collective to create Radio Alice, which began broadcasting on February 9, 1976, "under the sign of Aquarius." Bifo, Gomma, eds. *Alice è il diavolo, storia di una radio sovversiva*, Milan: Shake, 2002. The station took Enzo del Re's *Lavorare con lentezza (Work Slowly)* https://www.youtube.com/watch?v=3dwq3xPlVgU (last accessed July 4, 2014). as its theme song because Radio Alice was on "every day from 6:30 to 8:30 in the morning, so you could go to work happier, and from 2 p.m. to 2 a.m., so you could have something to do while waiting to go to work." Transcript of Radio Alice's first broadcast, in Bifo and Gomma, eds., *Alice è il diavolo. Storia di una radio sovversiva*, op. cit., p. 34. The first song on the air was *White Rabbit* by Jefferson Airplane, an homage to Lewis Carroll's Alice. A live broadcast interrupted the song: *"Go ask Alice, I think she'll know / When logic and proportion have fallen sloppy dead / And the white knight is talking backwards / And the red queen's off with her head.* Alice built a radio for herself, but in order to speak, she continues her daily fight against zombies and Jaberwockies." Ivi, p. 33.

The point was to wake up post-war Italy from its long Victorian slumber, to cross over to the other side of the mirror. In 1976, this was also suggested by English literature professor Gianni Celati, who introduced texts by Edward Lear and Lewis Carroll into the occupied Bologna University. The collective writing workshop Celati started would result in the novel *Alice disambientata (Alice Disoriented)*, again celebrating Carroll's infant character and its revival in the 1970s alternative culture: "Alice now appears everywhere. We see her in films, on the street, in dreams, in street demonstrations... In Wim Wenders's movie *Alice in the City*, it is Alice who sends the protagonist everywhere, she takes out money like a magician, allows the situation to develop, the journey to continue. The Radio Alice comrades have written: Alice is always someplace else." Gianni Celati, ed., *Alice disambientata*, Bologna, Le Lettere, 2007, p. 13.

In the seventies, radio became live and personal. The domestic sculpture that marked the hours of the day for Julie Kavener, Woody Allen's fictitious mother in *Radio Days* (1987), https://www.youtube.com/watch?v=xiolCtn1a4l (last accessed July 4, 2014). was stored away, and the transistor radio shifted the listening zone from the bourgeois living room to the private bedroom and outside to the street. In Nanni Moretti's *Ecce Bombo* (1978), Mario, seated on his bed, picks up the phone to call his favorite program and relate his personal reflection on the impossibility of an armed response to the Christian Democrats, since "the highway tunnels are too narrow for tanks." https://www.youtube.com/watch?v=ZMFig07pOo4 (last accessed July 4, 2014). In 1976 Fantozzi walks with his ear glued to the radio, to listen to news of the Italy—England soccer match. https://www.youtube.com/watch?v=o4Q6l-rhZses (last accessed July 4, 2014).
1977-radios were brought to strikes in order to follow the movements of the police after the murder of Francesco Lo Russo. https://www.youtube.com/watch?v=Hq6GbP7ipQ4&list=PLA628EA732FE7E226&index=13 (last accessed July 4, 2014). Protesters' phone calls to Radio Alice— eyewitness accounts of police violence on the

streets— provided live recordings of the temporary geography of an occupied Bologna. During that month of March, when Radio Alice shut down, Andrea Pazienza sent a new page of his *Pentothal* comic strip to *Linus*; the image of a radio dominated, exhorting people to gather, under a banner that reads "Francesco is alive and fights with us." In a note, Paz (as Pazienza was known) wrote: "While I was working on these pages, in February 1977, I was convinced that I was drawing a sudden ray of light, but I was sensationally mistaken, because it was, instead, a beginning."

Andrea Pazienza, *Le straordinarie avventure di Pentothal*, Roma, Fandango, 2010, p. 26.

This early personal use of the media contains the premises of a "one-many" form of communication that welcomes languages and voices of temporary communities and alternative narratives. The counterculture speaks out and enters a flow of widely disseminated information. In the hypothetical 1938 of *A Special Day* (1977), radio news about Hitler's visit to Mussolini pervades both the soundtrack of the film and the lives of the characters played by Marcello Mastroianni and Sophia Loren. Free radios, however, concentrated on minor voices and individual feelings that, until then, had been relegated to semi-private social spheres. https://www.youtube.com/watch?v=SmYMQcB8Mf0 (last accessed July 4, 2014). This movement from public to private brings to mind a mythic scene in the movie *Ecce Bombo* (1978), where Nanni Moretti, sitting in the kitchen, reads the newspaper headlines: "Andreotti: Italy is the freest nation in the world... The mayor gets the best of nudists: the police have expelled the hippy campers from

Santa Teresa di Gallura; the people were threatening insurrection. Trattorias open today: Amatrice, Lo Scipione…." A bell rings; Moretti lets out an anguished scream at an open window overlooking the rooftops of Rome. https://www.youtube.com/watch?v=ucTyli-arQ0 (last accessed July 4, 2014).

The history of free radio stations developed within the context of the State monopoly of communications, a situation that, in the early seventies, already seemed dated and authoritarian. While free radio stations sought to fragment the monolithic voice of the national stations, to make room for alternative visions, the independent broadcasting phenomenon, transposed into the realm of television, immediately took on a commercial tone. In 1979, Tele Milano, Berlusconi's first television channel, began broadcasting. Its operations were temporarily suspended in 1984 and reactivated in 1985, thanks to specially designed legislation. Decreto legge 20 ottobre 1984, n. 694, http://www.normattiva.it/uri-res/N2Ls?urn:nir:stato:decreto-legge:1984;694 (last accessed July 4, 2014). The relationship between public and private communications returned with the advent of the Internet in 1994, when the first Italian public Internet service began; called Iperbole, it was initially free but was soon assigned to private providers. Meanwhile, the anti-corruption initiative Mani Pulite (Operation Clean Hands) put in the media spotlight another form of communications control, the telephone interception, which raised other doubts about the public/private relationship. The 1980s dream of Congressman Mario in Ettora Scola's film *La terrazza*, who attempts to match public life and private reasons after having been the victim of a puritan press campaign, turned into the 1990s nightmare of a country obsessed with the politics of intimacy.

Twenty years after Radio Alice, the logic of free radio re-emerged with the actions of Luther Blissett, an anonymous collective personality that infiltrated the media like a virus and moved through television, the press, and other public spaces. Some of the members of the Luther Blissett project would later form Wu Ming, a writers' collective that Guido Chiesa involved in the screenplay for the film *Lavorare con lentezza* (*Working Slowly*), dedicated to the history of Radio Alice. Luther Blissett's first book, published in 1996, was titled *Totò, Peppino e la guerra psichica*. After Alice, the mutant child who was a symbol of "what I feel," Gianni Celati, ed., *Alice disambientata*, op.cit., p. 13. the new counterculture movements paid homage to the leading actor of "simulation and falsification, disguise and swindle, the decisive use of contemporary legends (…), a spectacular redemption, really a multiplication of identities." Luther Blissett, *Totò, Peppino e la guerra psichica*, Udine: AAA, 1996. Totò was a personality with multiple identities, someone who reacts to power with irony and comical force. In 1962, he played the Smemorato di Collegno (the Collegno Amnesiac) in the homonymous film by Sergio Corbucci. https://www.youtube.com/watch?v=4kvSiP6FbMo (last accessed July 4, 2014). Based on a true story from the 1920s, the film gives a portrait of a swindler caught robbing a vase in Turin's monumental cemetery. He feigns amnesia in order to avoid prison; nicknamed Smemorato, the amnesiac, he is confined to a mental hospital in Collegno, where he awaits identification. After his photo is published in the national papers, public opinion is split among those who hold one belief or another about his identity. The case inflames the Italian press for years, not lastly because it offers a compelling metaphor for the manipulation of information on the part of the Fascist regime. Leonardo Sciascia, *Il teatro della memoria; La sentenza memorabile*, Milan, Adelphi, 2004. The Amnesiac is a counter-manipulator who reveals the mechanisms of the control of communications. Luther Blissett also appropriated this dynamic in the 1990s, denouncing the disappearance of the fictitious artist Harry Kipper on the TV show *Chi l'ha visto? (Who saw him?)*, a forerunner of Italian reality TV. The artist was said to have disappeared along the border of the former Yugoslavia while trying to write the word "art" with his mountain bike.

FROM ITALY IN THE 60S TOWARDS THE 10S IN BRAZIL
Donatella Bernardi

Ten quotes from Carla Lonzi's *Autoritratto* [Self-Portrait], 1969, are associated with pictures. The first is a photographic collage addressing the myths in which Jesus as well as Buddha were created through ears and words. The nine others testify the activity of LapTopRadio in Brazil from August 28th until September 6th, 2012, following an invitation to contribute to Eternal Tour 2012 São Paulo. How can one inhabit the world? How can one travel and experience hospitality: to be welcomed and know how to welcome others? Experimentation of content and form is put into place, accompanied by a perpetual creolization motion, free from the trap of the definition of being or of origins. As an unconscious tribute to Lonzi's methodology and vision (love, creativity, creation, empowerment, self-definition of art, and its practice vs. culture), we had just started to record a conversation some years ago in a given time and space. The sovereignty of the media helps to concentrate on the present moment. The flux of voices and sounds follows our desire for collective and creative endeavors supported by strong self-reflectivity and intense internal dialogue.

[Carla] Accardi: [...] I was telling you the other day coming back from the sea, it's not as if you can have more than two or three great loves in life, just like that. Why? Because if the sense of repeating certain experiences comes too quickly, as a matter of maturity, and as a matter of oneself evolving with time, you can't handle it. If you enter further into anomaly, into Don Juanism, you know, things that I've read of every so often, that's how it is. So, let's look a bit at the typology of a person who goes down a particular path over the course of seventy years... A person must live several years as a child, learn to walk, learn to eat. Then you learn to compare yourself to others, yet free yourself from the hazards of youth at the same time... then comes a powerful moment of creativity, let's say between the ages of twenty and thirty, when you hastily jot down notes. Because you have truly opened your eyes, you see, and you scribble these notes, with such aggressiveness... Then, between thirty and forty you dedicate yourself to something, and... you then maintain the pleasure of work that comes from beauty, but always listening to others, to what happens around you... Perhaps later on, even if you close yourself off in the studio, you begin to see yourself somewhat from the outside to which you pay so much mind, you see?

[...] Oh, [one] night I had a truly vital moment, and I don't know where, I read this thing about creativity. Oh yes, the points of high consciousness, I don't know, that you reach in many ways through life, either in orgasm or in creativity, in contemplation, or doing something for someone you love, something that is good for them, I don't know... Anyhow, I remind myself that these things are never lost. pp. 71–73 De Donato Editore 1969

[Carla] Lonzi: Today we can be close to artists, listening and even re-listening afterward if we didn't understand them at first. [...] The first time I used a tape recorder, I thought, "What is happening?" I didn't understand it very well, and I truly felt strange using this tape recorder, since it's not such an easy a thing to get used to. So then I said, "Well, it's logical that he meant to say this," that is, that I want to stay close to artists and free myself, as someone who can take part in university culture... Because the funny thing is that the critic, when learning what the artist is, learns it at university and learns it in historical texts. This is then his concept of the artist, and he will never dispute culture or critique again—never again, with or without a recorder. I like these works of yours because when I'm there inside, I feel like any other person, without all the protection of culture, of privilege, that I need if I go, say, to a museum. But there, I'm really—how do I put it? I'm like a person who goes into a church because, I don't know, there's a problem that her own culture isn't resolving for her in any way... a person very skeptical of the regular sensations that people have and of her own special ability to perceive.

pp. 79—80 De Donato Editore 1969

[Jannis] Kounellis: [...] the work of a painter is to liberate an object without imposing reason onto it. If he does impose himself, he has liberated a thing, but not a person. Whatever the cost, the artist must remain truly still and not approach it with violence. If he does not, he may be accepted, perhaps, but he will never be understood, or he will be vaguely understood... He won't become vital, while a painting has a truly vital, extreme significance, and this must be understood. The depths of the painting must be understood, helping to liberate and understand. What other meaning can a painting have? p. 128 De Donato Editore 1969

[Luciano] Fabro: I indeed think that now, where there exists a vitality, a touch of vitality, this avoidance is quite natural. That is to say that it works so long as you succeed in eluding among us artists who do a certain kind of work. You manage to stay alive so long as, little by little, you manage to get out of the way, to proceed as if these catalogues and files didn't exist. Little by little... It's the work of another, someone who constantly finds himself having to revise these files because he's noticed that they were previously put in the wrong order. p. 92 De Donato Editore 1969

[Carla] Lonzi: What in recording attracts me personally? I'm very much attracted to an elementary fact of it: the ability to pass from certain sounds to punctuation, to writing, finding a page that is not a written page, but a page that... In other words, as with chemical processes, when there's condensation... from a sound a sign condenses, that's it, like liquid coming from the gas state. I like it very much, though I couldn't say why... and I love being able to read something different from what you usually read, always produced by a labor of the brain, so tiresome to think of now. [...] I've noticed, many times, with things I've recorded that seemed boring or something, that you can't imagine what they become afterword. Even a comma becomes irremovable, because I really have a reverence for what happened, with everything that it implies. Just the meager fact implies all, you see? It will recall something so one-note that it drives me insane... then, once I listen to it, I can't take anything out. pp. 39—41

De Donato Editore 1969

[Carla] Accardi: In many books there is this anguish felt by the man—the scholar, the sage, the philosopher—for not being able to resolve something or give an explicit answer. This is something I certainly consider... natural, to which I yield, really, as something extraordinary. He has it at all levels: Man wants to find a career in a finite way, or otherwise he wants to conquer a people with complete authority, or he wants to arrive at a conclusive reasoning to explain a problem... And for this, he endures suffering that, if he doesn't succeed, brings him either to the brink of madness or to the wisdom that many have… The sage, really, the sage detached from everything for having had to give up, always holds onto the fact that he had to quit. You do not find this in Woman… Vitality, naturally, has kept the woman at a level close to the ground up to now, don't you think? To polish the floors and cook because she, poor thing, had the instinct for it. pp. 154–155 De Donato Editore 1969

[Pietro] Consagra: All in all, the artist invests himself as a worker, invests himself as a sufferer, as someone experiencing joy, as someone in love, as a sailor… and he sees all of these roles as those of artists. He then sets himself to a given task, akin to a recognition of this thing happening around him, if you will. Yet when he sees all of the little characters that for him truly create this invented thing… That is to say that the artist is like an idiot, all things considered, because if he were more intelligent, more than what he is, he could just fail to bring his concept to fruition, thinking that everyone else is already an artist in his or her own right. But the artist does realize his goal, continues to create more work, and pieces together the mechanics of his work… So for me, the most exciting thing is that discovery, why the artist works, what the mechanism is by which the artist forces himself to work, rather than seeking to put off projects and entering into other things without having reached anything. But he wants to realize something;

there is that pleasure: what is this pleasure in speaking and reasoning through what he does? pp. 171–172 De Donato Editore 1969

[Carla] Lonzi: However, there is a variation on this theme, and I'd like to record it, now that it comes to mind: indeed, one could say that a woman lacks the incentive to create because she is already a producer of life, bearing children, a fact obscured by excrement in her consciousness, a debilitating fact of humanity. When, therefore, a woman sets out to do something creative—I'm already touching on this nerve, but I love it—she has a slightly different attitude from that of a man, not achieving the need for sublimation, to truly, completely disconnect... but it's something very much connected to her own essence... This is a possible hypothesis, but now we must see if women will create and how, in a more extensive case than the current one... Certainly, women have had difficulty accepting creativity in very sublimate masculine terms. They strike them as a bit unnatural, feeling heavily forced. [...]

[Salvatore] Scarpitta: [...] I've wanted to remove the hermetic and hygienic from my work, to return in the direction of a particular intimacy that one has in coprophagia or playing around with shit—as a contrast, really—or more specifically in my case, bitumen, oil, oily bandages, things dirtied by an organic world. pp. 184–186 De Donato Editore 1969

[Pino] Pascali: I try to do what I like to do, and in the end it's the only system that works for me. I don't think that a sculptor's work is overbearing: he plays, as anyone who does what he wants plays. It's not as if play is only for children—everything is a game, isn't it? p. 195 De Donato Editore 1969.

[Pietro] Consagra: You become an artist when every experience that you have is a personal issue, and when you scrutinize every piece of information that you receive according to your own personality, based on your very freedom: you cultivate a great awareness of yourself. This doesn't mean that the artist is an egoist; here egocentrism has no significance because the artist, in this case, is a man who also suffers much, who is living all possible experiences... corresponding by nature, of course, to a selection of his: one artist is able to create certain experiences, and another artist is able to create other experiences just as, of course, any man has qualities that not everyone possesses. Now, a person becomes an artist little by little, bit by bit, nurturing this awareness of making every fact personal, an experience within himself. To what does this lead? To the fact that each of us, every artist, likens himself to one

Cirurgia poética [Poetic surgery] by Dominique Fleury and Ana Texeira and LapTopRadio, Eternal Tour 2012 São Paulo. Image: Boris Meister.

of these tape recordings, as someone who collects experiences... And he needs these experiences to have a record ready of what has happened around him. The artist is thus always contemporary to the life of a man: he identifies himself as a person, more than any other individual, with what he does. [...] It follows that the artist is the least disconnected individual of all. Now there is a great susceptibility in this lack of disconnection: in this case, the artist is the most vulnerable of all possible men [...] pp. 232–233 De Donato Editore 1969

SELF-PORTRAIT OF A WOMAN—CARLA LONZI'S *AUTORITRATTO*

Giovanna Zapperi

Translated from French by Jason Francis Mc Gimsey. Previously published in French: "L'autoportrait d'une femme. Préface." In Carla Lonzi, *Autoportrait*, translated from Italian by Marie-Ange Marie-Vigueur, edited and prefaced by Giovanna Zapperi, Paris-Zurich, JRP Ringier, 2012, pp. 7–35. The in-text citations have been translated by Jason Francis Mc Gimsey from the original Italian version of Carla Lonzi, Autoritratto, Milan, et al. Edizioni, 2010.

BETWEEN ART CRITICISM AND RADICAL FEMINISM

The publication of *Autoritratto* [Self-Portrait] in the summer of 1969, marks the culminating point of Carla Lonzi's activity as an art critic after a decade spent at the heart of the Italian artistic scene as a critic and curator. This publication also signals her break—abrupt but explicit in the book's pages—with the art world: in 1970, the first manifesto of *Rivolta Femminile* [Feminine Revolt], the feminist collective that she had founded earlier that year, would appear. From that moment on, Lonzi dedicated all her energy to feminism, where she would quickly become a central figure. *Autoritratto* showed Lonzi's deep dissatisfaction with art criticism, which she considered to be a fundamentally authoritarian and inauthentic activity. We could even say that this volume is a virulent attack on art criticism as it was practiced in Italy at the time.

The book is made up of a series of interviews with artists, carried out between 1965 and 1969, that were first recorded, then transcribed, and finally recomposed in a textual montage where nothing of the *continuum* of the original exchanges remains. With her fragmented transcriptions, Lonzi associates a series of images whose role in the book isn't to merely illustrate the text. The relation between the texts and the images is clearly more complex, drawing an affective geography where artwork reproductions mix with intimate images. Her use of montage, oral expression, exchange, and sharing make *Autoritratto* a significantly experimental book, deeply driven by the tension that motivated Lonzi at that time: the tension between her desire to give up her authority as an art critic and to find an authorial position able to reinvent itself based on that rejection. *Autoritratto*, already from the title, puts the I of the author at the center but does so starting from a horizontal, non-hierarchical relation with the other voices— those of the artists—woven throughout the book. The attempt to undo art criticism in favor of the artist's spoken words and the moment of creation is compared to the act of arranging images and texts, words and writing, relations and affects. After its publication in 1969, this book was for a long period forgotten, until the recent republication Carla Lonzi, *Autoritratto*, Milan, ed. et al., 2010, with an introduction by Laura Iamurri. The original edition was published by De Donato (Bari) in 1969. Until recent editions, Carla Lonzi's writings circulated essentially among feminists. of Carla Lonzi's writings on art and feminism. The fact that she had abandoned art criticism probably played a crucial role in this oversight, but, in any case, she had barely occupied a marginal position in a world that was still chiefly dominated by men (both artists and critics). This art world was also guided by an idea of art that focused on grand narratives, a notion feminist critique has never stopped deconstructing since: the myth of genius and originality, the autonomy of artwork and its supposed neutrality. Linda Nochlin's "founding" text, where the American art historian starts a feminist critique of the categories reigning over artistic creation, will be published in 1971; see L. Nochlin, "Why Have There Been No Great Women Artists?" *In Women, Art, and Power and Other Essays*, Boulder, Colorado, Westview Press, 1988, pp 147–158. With the exception of Germano Celant's late recognition of her work on the occasion of the *Identité Italienne* [Italian Identity] exhibition in 1981 Celant had asked Carla Lonzi to write a catalogue essay for the exhibition he was organizing at Paris' Centre Pompidou. In the short, untitled text that she gave him, she discussed her past engagements and reaffirmed her reasons for distancing herself. See G. Celant (dir.), *Identité Italienne. L'art en Italie depuis 1959*, Paris, Musée National d'Art Moderne, Centre Georges Pompidou, 1981, p. 31 at Centre Georges Pompidou in Paris and the posthumous homage dedicated to her by the Venice Biennale in 1993, Anne-Marie Sauzeau was at the origin of this homage. See A. Sauzeau, "Omaggio a Carla Lonzi." *In XLV Esposizione Internazionale d'Arte*, vol. 1, Venice, Biennale di Venezia, 1993, pp. 36–37. eleven years after her death, Lonzi's role in the history of art criticism went largely unexplored for many decades. Only at the end of the first decade of the 21st century did a new generation of scholars take interest in her writings, trying to update the possible connection between a feminist history of art in Italy and a history of Italian feminism. Among the recent publications, see: Lara Conte, Vinzia Fiorino, Vanessa Martini (dir.), *Carla Lonzi: la duplice radicalità. Dalla critica miltante al femminismo di Rivolta, Pisa, ETS, 2011; Maria Antonietta Tras-forini (dir.), Donne d'arte. Storie e generazioni, Rome, Meltemi, 2006; Martina Corgnati, Artiste. Dall'Impressionismo al nuovo millennio, Milan, Bruno Mondadori, 2004, pp. 278–307.* In France, Fulvia Carnevale recently published "Sputiamo su Hegel" in a contemporary art review (with a group of texts from Italian feminism), see: MAY, n. 4, 6/2010.

Carla Lonzi's name has remained etched in Italian history mostly for her work in feminism, while the importance of her activity as an art critic only began to emerge after enough time had passed to make her art criticism intelligible through the feminist reframing of her historical context.

A Hemisfair, San Antonio, Texas 1968

This effort to reframe her work cannot settle for the (indispensable) reevaluation of her writings; as Griselda Pollock writes, it isn't about adding the names of forgotten women to a ready-made history, but of reformulating history itself—its phallocentrism, its ideological implications—from a gendered perspective. Griselda Pollock, *Encounters in the Virtual Feminist Museum. Time, Space, and the Archive*, London, Routledge, 2007, pp. 9–25. In this sense, reading *Autoritratto* in a feminist perspective doesn't mean situating it exclusively in relation to Carla Lonzi's feminism—whether in terms of a rupture or, on the contrary, a prefiguration. What matters is trying to identify what ties this work to art history as a gendered domain, to woman's history and women writers, and to the history of feminism. We might say that rediscovering Carla Lonzi as an art critic shares the same—discontinuous and nonlinear—timeline that characterizes the rediscovering of woman artists who have punctuated prestigious international exhibitions over the last decade or so. On this point, see Elisabeth Lebovici and Giovanna Zapperi, "Découvertes excitantes. Emplois et contre-emplois du féminisme dans les expositions," Multitudes, n. 31, 2008, pp. 191–200.

So, although Lonzi's activity as an art critic has been long held back, her name still evokes the history of Italian feminism, of which she was one of the most noteworthy figures: in 1970, Carla Lonzi founded the *Rivolta Femminile* collective with her friend Carla Accardi, the only woman artist that participated in the *Autoritratto* conversations. Throughout *Rivolta Femminile*'s first years, Lonzi wrote a handful of striking texts (often signed collectively, even if she had been the author), including the legendary "*Sputiamo su Hegel*" [Let's Spit on Hegel], a ferocious deconstruction of the master-slave dialectic and class struggle that, in her opinion, participate in patriarchy. The echo provoked by this text, associated with her charismatic personality, meant that she would soon occupy a central position in the history of Italian feminism. As Liliana Ellena remarks, Lonzi's own work abetted in transforming her into an icon, which has rendered a historical reconstruction of her trajectory difficult: her 1970 texts are actually considered the origin of Italian feminism. Liliana Ellena, "Carla Lonzi e il neo-femminismo radicale degli anni '70: disfare la cultura, disfare la politica." In L. Conte et al., *Carla Lonzi: la duplice radicalità*, op. cit., pp. 119–121. It may seem surprising, but this idea has erased the tie between the beginnings of the feminist movement and the domain of the visual arts. This erasure is above all linked to Carla Lonzi's own idea about her past as an art critic, since she often stressed in the pages of her diary how much feminism was a beginning for her, a way of demanding "the right to start from scratch." Carla Lonzi, *Taci, anzi parla. Diario di una femminista*, Milan, Scritti di Rivolta Femminile, 1978, p. 41, August 14, 1972 (new edition: Milan, et al./edizioni, 2010) [our translation]. Lonzi experienced feminism as a chance for self-expression and a political awareness that she had not found alongside artists. Feminism, she wrote, "was my party. Ivi, p. 44 [our translation]."

While Lonzi's path from art to feminism may seem sporadic, reading her art criticism through feminist epistemology allows us to recognize a complexity that the idea of a clean break between art and feminism prevents us from noticing. This complexity can also be detailed with the numerous elements that lead to a bleed through between her writings on art and those on feminism, beginning from the discursive approaches and the forms of writing that she adopted. In her feminist writings, Lonzi uses artistic avant-garde methods: the use of the manifesto form, assertoric language, and her use of a collective subjectivity—that "us" that constitutes both the subject of the discourse and its recipient. These elements are a clear call back to the style used in Futurist manifestos. Moreover, Lonzi's first feminist texts show a creative approach to writing where conflict and the continual transgression of gender limits are expressed. For example, the expression "Let's Spit on Hegel" harkens back to an aggressive act that, in Italy at that time, could only be done by men.

We could even say that *Autoritratto* uses the main features of feminine and feminist literature: self narrative, the importance of subjectivity, and the pleasure of conversation can be interpreted, following Irit Rogoff's suggestion, as many approaches that pave the way for an alternative, feminist, and gendered history of art through a series of small-scale actions that sit at the margins. Irit Rogoff, "Gossip as Testimony. A Postmodern Signature." In G. Pollock (dir.), *Generations and Geographies in the Visual Arts. Feminist Readings*, London, Routledge, 1996, p. 77. The forms practiced in *Autoritratto* will be used again (and transformed) by Carla Lonzi in the 1970s, especially in the feminist practice of *autocoscienza*—an Italian version of *consciousness raising* of American import—focused on exchange and conversation, as well as in her diary writing between 1972 and 1977. Private diary writing indeed marks a new phase for Lonzi after her 1970–72 writings, collected in a book in 1974: Carla Lonzi, *Sputiamo su Hegel e altri scritti, Milano, Scritti di Rivolta Femminile*, 1974 (new edition: Milan, et al./ edizioni, 2010). From this point of view, the feminist awareness at the end of the 1960s is not simply the point of no return of a long personal crisis but also the beginning of a future where creative practice and political engagement mingle.

Lonzi's transformation into a legendary figure, to an irreducible singularity, has most likely contributed to making this complexity hard to see, coupled with the difficulty of

reading her texts on art in the larger context of femi-
nine and feminist writings in Italy in the 1960s and
1970s. This question is the object of an essay by Judith Russi
Kirshner dedicated to Carla Lonzi, Lea Vergine, and Anne-Marie
Sauzeau—two feminist art critics active in Italy in the 1960s and
1970s—in the wider context of Italian feminism. J. Russi Kirshner,
"Voices and Images of Italian Feminism." In Connie Butler (dir.),
WACK! Art and the Feminist Revolution, cat. exp. Los Angeles,
Museum of Contemporary Art, Cambridge, Mass., MIT Press,
2007, pp. 384–399. Lonzi's particular status in Italian
feminism has to do with the search for the origins
where current feminist struggles' self-representation
and the importance of the controversial question of the
genealogy in Italian feminism are both at stake. Yet,
the gap between these practices, the narrations and
histories of feminism and art can not only be understood in the terms of a delay or a difficulty of reconstructing Lonzi's path, but also as a simultaneously
contradictory and productive place. The different time
periods when Carla Lonzi's writings were received also show the relevance of her thought for future generations of feminists.

A FRAGMENTED SUBJECT

Autoritratto was written based on
interviews that Carla Lonzi conducted with fourteen
artists, all credited in the book's subtitle: Accardi,
Alviani, Castellani, Consagra, Fabro, Fontana, Kounellis,
Nigro, Paolini, Pascali, Rotella, Scarpitta, Turcato,
and Twombly. A handful of these interviews had already been published (in part or whole) in exhibition

catalogues or in the review *Marcatré*, where Carla Lonzi wrote a section called "Discorsi" [Discourses] from 1966 on. In her short preface, Lonzi dates the various conversations between 1965 and 1969, specifying that she had interviewed most of the artists more than once (with the exception of Fontana, Pascali, Rotella, Scarpitta, and Twombly). Lonzi did a large part of the transcription and montage work during a long visit to the United States, where her partner, the artist Pietro Consagra, had been invited to teach a semester at the Minneapolis School of Art On Lonzi's American trip, see Anna Jaquinta and Marta Lonzi, *Vita di Carla Lonzi*, Milan, Scritti di Rivolta Femminile, 1990, pp. 21–23. in the autumn of 1967 and spring of 1968. In her introduction, visibly penned just before submitting the text to her editors, Lonzi wrote that these conversations with artists were, essentially, a way of connecting— "of conversing with someone in a largely communicative and humanly satisfying way" (p. 3)—as a way of accepting, collectively, the invitation to participate that, for her, was the scope of art itself. Exchange instead of interpretation, giving the floor to artists rather than explaining the reasons and the meaning of their work, are the ways that Lonzi unravels the art critic's authority. However, she also does so in order to find a different role for herself, a role where creativity wouldn't be kept at arm's length as an object of study.

This collective dimension is also at the heart of the book's composition. Lonzi uses montage as a means to make the artists' dialogue amongst themselves, often through thematic sequences that juxtapose exchanges regarding one topic or another tied to the current artistic or political events at that time. We could say that this tactic is planned, explicitly, from the first page, when Lonzi invites all the participants together in an imaginary scene that immediately stresses the multiplication of voices and the strongly subjective dimension that gives the book its title, where "each artist speaks for themselves, in the first person, and speaks about themselves, about their work and their existence. Laura Iamurri, "Prefazione." In Carla Lonzi, *Autoritratto*, op. cit., p. VII [our translation]."

The conversations continue around the work of each artist, their careers, and their expositions; they uncondescendingly examine the difficulties encountered by artists in the 1960s and the critical debates of that decade. Larger questions—the 1968 revolts, women's conditions, and the Black American struggles for civil rights or political and cultural life in Italy at the time—all occupy an important place in the text. In this way, it opens a unique door to the whole epoch, an entire generation, and a precise social and geographic context.

In this uninterrupted conversation, Carla Lonzi is one of the characters in the book: she speaks up to express her opinion on the topics addressed in the same way the artists do; she rarely poses questions, privileging listening and participation. She never gives interpretations of what the artists say: in this sense, she doesn't mediate but has exchanges that are more like conversations where roles are not clearly established. In particular, Lonzi speaks many times about the reasons that led her to record the interviews and her discontent with working as a critic. She specifically defends the authenticity of her relationship to the artists against the idea that art criticism should be a form of mediation that intellectualizes art and neutralizes its potentially transformative reach. The critic, Lonzi declares, is "obsessed" (p. 16): they insist on transforming what arises first and foremost from experience—and thus from life itself—into institutionalized knowledge. Art criticism is therefore a deformation of the artist's work (p. 24), the fruit of an "unnatural" effort—in other words, an obsession (p. 29). On the contrary, picking up a tape recorder and recording conversations consequently becomes an act of liberation: participation replaces intellectual control.

In the pages of *Autoritratto*, Lonzi especially picks a bone with art critics' training in a context where art critics were often also scholars. If one considers that Lonzi herself had been a student of Roberto Longhi, one of the most influential art historians of the time, this attack against art criticism as institutionalized knowledge also represents a radical questioning of her own life. Lonzi, who had been a brilliant student, hadn't wanted to pursue a university career After graduating, Lonzi will not follow up on Longhi's proposal to publish her thesis, defended in 1956. See Anna Jaquinta and Marta Lonzi, *Vita di Carla Lonzi*, op. cit., p. 12. This work would finally be published posthumously: Carla Lonzi, *Rapporti tra la scena e le arti figurative dalla fine dell'Ottocento*, Moreno Bucci (ed.), Florence, Leo S. Olschki Editore, 1995.: in one conversation, she refers back to this choice, explaining that "for me, the university wasn't satisfying, I mean, it was a bureaucratic fact, a cultural fact, and a rather repressive one" (p.32). Lonzi will develop these reflections on the repressive character of university education in her feminist writings; in "*Sputiamo su Hegel*," she specifically writes that, for a young woman, the university "is not the place for liberation through culture" but one much more akin to "a repression, if well cultivated in the framework of the family." Carla Lonzi, *Sputiamo su Hegel*, op. cit., p. 43 [our translation]. Despite her choice to work with contemporary art, she remained in contact with her ex-mentor for a long time, notably through her long collaboration at *L'Approdo*, a radio program and review of general culture where Longhi directed the visual arts section. Carla Lonzi was a regular collaborator with *L'Approdo*; she maintained a bimonthly column there throughout the 1960s even though her relations with Longhi were tense starting in 1963 until their definitive rupture in 1969. On this aspect of her activity, see Michela Baldini, "Le arti figurative all'Approdo. Carla Lonzi: un'allieva dissidente di Roberto Longhi," *Italianistica*, vol. XXXVIII, n. 3, 2009, pp. 115–131; Vanessa Martini, "La collaborazione di Carla Lonzi alla rubrica Arti Figurative de 'L'Approdo'." In Lara Conte, Laura Iamurri, and Vanessa Martini (eds.), *Carla Lonzi, Scritti sull'arte*, Milan, et al., 2012, pp. 669–684. Carla Lonzi had received a classical education at the University of Florence, where a positivist spirit focused on monographs characterized the department of art history, adopting the objectivity of vision as an epistemological foundation. Roberto Longhi's method was particularly based on the visual evidence of artwork and on the importance of style more than its historical and cultural contextualization. Roberto Longhi (1890–1970) is a central figure in art history in Italy; he was a professor at the University of Bologna (1934–1948) and then Florence (from 1949), an art critic, and founder of the reviews *Proporzioni* (1943) and *Paragone* (1950). He is notably the author of essays on Piero della Francesca, Caravaggio, and Boccioni. A very influential teacher (among others, Pasolini was one of his students), he developed an innovative style of writing that was even compared to that of Carlo Emilio Gadda. In particular, see Giovanni Previtali (dir.), *L'arte di scrivere sull'arte. Roberto Longhi e la cultura del nostro tempo*, Rome, Editori Riuniti, 1982 and Ezio Raimondi, *Barocco moderno. Roberto Longhi and Carlo Emilio Gadda*, Milan, Mondadori, 2003. On the relations between Carla Lonzi and Roberto Longhi, see: Vanessa Martini, "Gli inizi della 'straordinaria stagione' di Carla Lonzi: 1953–1963." In L. Conte, V. Fiorino, V. Martini (dir.), *Carla Lonzi: la duplice radicalità*, op. cit., pp. 11–43. Compared to that model, *Autoritratto* is a resolutely undisciplined and anti-disciplinary book, especially because it abandons the monographic format—centered on the artist's uniqueness—in favor of a scattering of the artist in an array of often discordant voices.

From this viewpoint, a crucial stage of Lonzi's detachment from the intellectual institutions where she had been educated takes place when she chooses to privilege the spoken word over observation. The passage from writing to audio recording means shifting the objectivity of the art historian's writing to a more subjective dimension, a move that will be vital in her later passage to feminism. Producing knowledge through the language of art criticism, something Lonzi had done for so many years, started looking like the production of dead knowledge to her because it was incapable of experiencing the present. Giving up the form of objective knowledge based on vision, and therefore a form of detachment, in favor of a form of subjective engagement, based on words and participation, may represent Lonzi's most radical attempt to rethink the very structures through which culture produces knowledge.

At the center of this radical reassessment, we see the art critic and the authority of observation, the fact of being outside of things, of commenting on them instead of absorbing them (p. 35). While the critical impulse, writes Lonzi, is born from a need or an individual temperament to "intrude on other people's situations" (p. 33), only later does this temperament come back to an institutionalized and hierarchical form of knowledge: "The critic, instead of being someone who is available and who needs, becomes someone who judges and creates a whole hierarchy. And in the activity that a critic ends up exercising, they really cancel out the thing they started off from and the critic becomes inauthentic, with no more authenticity" (p. 34).

In Lonzi's vocabulary, the idea of authenticity means the ability of being with, and not beside, things—a skill that she attributes to artists. So, it is no coincidence that Lonzi calls out to artists to destroy the role of art criticism in the name of radical subjectivation of experiential knowledge. As she clearly writes in a letter on January 12th, 1969, addressed to the editor-in-chief of L'Approdo, "I don't so much do art criticism—an abuse of society that mythicizes art and, at the same time, is afraid of it—as rather experience of the sense of art. Letter published by M. Baldini, op. cit., p. 125 [our translation]." So, giving up the objectivity of writing also means breaking the bounds that separate the artist from the critic, the artwork from the spectator, the author from the reader. We are left with a fragmented subject and a textual agency where the role of the author is drawn taut by the techniques of recording and montage.

In her preface, Lonzi explains that she didn't conduct the interviews with the goal of making a book and that what interested her in the use of a tape recorder was the possibility of transforming her activity as a critic. Recording, transcribing, and re-experiencing the words through writing were necessary acts in her attempt to reinvent her relationship to art so that it wasn't centered on the repressive power of interpretation. In reality, challenging art criticism keeps Lonzi busy for the whole decade, starting from her first article in 1963, "*La Solitudine del critico*" ["The Solitude of the Art Critic"], Carla Lonzi, "La Solitudine del critico" In *Scritti sull'arte*, op. cit., pp. 353–356 (this article originally appeared in *L'Avanti!*, December 13, 1963). Lonzi wrote this text in response to the positions expressed by the influential art critic and historian Giulio Carlo Argan at the *XII Convegno internazionale Artisti, Critici, Studiosi d'arte* [the 12th International Conference of Artists, Art Critics, and Art Historians] held in Verucchio. On the debate that followed this event, in particular see Lara Conte, "La critica è potere. Percorsi e momenti della critica italiana." In L. Conte et al. (dir.), *Carla Lonzi : la duplice radicalità*, op. cit., pp. 87–93. where she already lays the groundwork for the arguments developed in her "zero degrees of silence, Lara Conte, "Carla Lonzi a Torino: alcune coordinate." In *Carla Lonzi, Scritti sull'arte*, op. cit., p. 702 [our translation]." and in her insistence of giving voice to artists. She goes all the way until withdrawing completely from art criticism in 1970, made clear in one of her last critical texts, fittingly entitled "*La critica è potere*" ["Art Criticism is Power"]. Carla Lonzi, "La critica è potere." In *Scritti sull'arte*, op. cit., pp. 647–650 (this article originally appeared in *NAC. Notiziario Arte Contemporanea*, n. s., n. 3, December 1970, pp. 5–6). However, Lonzi's withdrawal was not linear since she continued to work with *L'Approdo* until 1969, where, despite her more and more serious differences with her ex-mentor, she continued to write art criticism in a classic style, far from the experiments that she achieved in other contexts.

Her *Autoritratto* is just like the questioning of the role of the author and the authority of interpretation Susan Sontag's celebrated essay "Against Interpretation" was originally published in 1966; see Susan Sontag, *Against Interpretation: And Other Essays*, London, Picador, 2001. The essay can be found online at: http://www.uiowa.edu/~c08g001d/Sontag_AgainstInterp.pdf, [consulted 10 August 2014]. common in critical thinking at the time. In this sense, Lonzi's work echoes Roland Barthes' "The Death of the Author," published in 1968, when he wrote "it is language which speaks, not the author Roland Barthes, "The Death of the Author." In *Image-Music-Text*, translated by Stephen Heath, New York, Hill and Wang, 1978, p. 143.", or when he describes the text as "a multidimensional space in which are married and contested several writings, none of which is original: the text is a fabric of quotations, resulting from a thousand sources of culture. Ivi, pp. 145–146."

Likewise, Lonzi's reinvented authorial position starts from the dispersal of the text she recomposes, searching for a production of sense that is not the authoritarian I but the expression of a multiple and fragmented subject. The text seen as a quilt of interwoven citations particularly lends itself to a description of how the book was made because it is the result of a montage, a technique like cutting and sewing patches into new patterns. It is no coincidence if Barthes' critique, followed by Foucault's shortly thereafter, Michel Foucault, "What is an Author?" (1969). In *The Foucault Reader*, New York, Pantheon Books, 1984, pp. 101–119. openly agrees with the disappearance of the author, already decreed by avant-garde literature.

At the heart of the poststructuralist critique of the author, we also find the myth of intentionality, of the literary work as expression of the I of its author. From this viewpoint, what is troubling about Lonzi's work is the consistent paradox on one hand of undoing her own position as author/art critic and, on the other, of reasserting the myths of intention and the expression of the self as inherent features of the artist. Her insistence on the notion of an artist's authenticity suggests a powerful form of identification, at the limits of mimesis, with artists. At that precise moment, her closeness to the artists served her as a way of escaping her own alienation as a critic in search of a creative form of writing about art able to reinvent the relation between the artist and society and founded on recognizing art's authenticity. C. Lonzi, "La critica è potere," op. cit.

This idea of art as the expression of the artist's authenticity was, however, in crisis at the end of the 1960s and, actually, the work of women artists began to analyze the notion of author inherited from western tradition as a masculine myth. So we might wonder why Lonzi completely questions herself—her role, her trade, and her intellectual and professional paths—and reconfigures everything starting from a relation with the artist, to whom she awards the gift of embodying the authenticity that she feels is compromised in art criticism. The answer probably lies in the importance of subjectivity, which is, for Lonzi, always gendered. This is what she will specify later in the pages of her diary, when she goes back over her closeness with the artists and the importance of thinking of herself as subject of her own trajectory: "*Rivolta Femminile* was created by two people, Ester Ester is a pseudonym for Carla Accardi. In her diary, Carla Lonzi changed all the names of her friends and myself, who interrogated themselves on masculine subjectivity because we saw ourselves as subjects: Ester as an artist, and myself as aware of my 'different' identity. Carla Lonzi, *Taci, anzi parla,* op. cit., p. 40 (14 August 1972) [our translation]." This awareness of a different identity, one she cannot clearly name, marks on one hand her dis-identification with the profession and the figure of the art critic, while, on the other, she signals a potentially new condition of a becoming subject.

In fact, as several feminist theorists have highlighted, the author whose death was decreed in 1968 is male, For example, see Kaja Silverman, *The Acoustic Mirror. The Female Voice in Psychoanalysis and Cinema*, Bloomington, Indiana University Press, 1988, pp. 191 and following. and the same goes for the figure of the art critic that Lonzi couldn't identify with. So, her attempt to reinvent an author's position in her *Autoritratto* experiment shouldn't be read in the retrospective light of Lonzi's feminism, but rather in the framework of a gendered interpretation of the roles that she tried not only to undo but also to rebuild. We might say that the tension between the end of art criticism and the beginning of an authentic position is tinged with a conflict that must be read through the prism of gender since "the death of the author" meant something completely different for women. On one hand, the end of the author as the embodiment of male dominance went in the direction of a feminist critique of the phallocentrism of the system of art and its institutions. On the other hand, being an author could mean something completely different for a woman, above all if we think about that role from the viewpoint of a becoming subject. This question is clearly at the heart of the feminist critique of art history. See the pioneering book by Roszika Parker and Griselda Pollock, *Old Mistresses. Women, Art, and Ideology*, London, Pandora, 1981. In the feminisms of the 1970s, subjectivity is a crucial question for examining forms of female agency. The tension in Lonzi's critical texts thus surfaces as a specific kind of self-invention, liberation, and female resistance. Along the path that led Lonzi to step back from the epistemological structures she had been educated in, her relation with artists is where the process of her own subjectivation is played out. That process, as we now know, is also a goodbye: *Autoritratto* ended up compromising her possibility of working from inside any standard cultural and artistic framework. With feminism, which Lonzi describes as the eruption of an "Unexpected Subject" Carla Lonzi, *Sputiamo su Hegel*, op. cit., p. 47. into the world, this process finds another path.

ART AND POLITICS

In *Autoritratto*, we follow the conversations with each of the different artists cited in the title, Cy Twombly's silence being the only exception. Lonzi had actually sent him a series of questions in 1962, but he never answered; she decided to keep the questions in the book anyway, followed by his silence.

The academic style, full of scholarly references to art history, of the questions reminds us of Lonzi's university training. Keeping these answerless questions lets us see the process that led Lonzi to disengage from— that is, unravel—the intellectual attitudes of the language that would still be in vogue in Italian art history departments for a long time to come. As she mentions in her preface, these questions "are still colored by my precedent attitude regarding the artist [...] they carry the echo of an academic, but graceful, language" (p. 6). So, the change in tone seen between the 1962 questions and the other parts of the text shows that the conversation montage entails a layered timescale, and that, in a way, the reader actually meets Carla Lonzi in different moments of the 1960s.

The questions sent to Cy Twombly also play a special role in the textual balance because he is the only American artist in the book. Cy Twombly moved to Rome in 1959. Plus, despite the failure interview and the differences in tone and method in respect to the others, the fact that these questions were formulated in 1962 shows Lonzi's early interest in dialogue. A short while later (from 1965, when she first recorded with Fabro), this will lead her to formulate her concerns about the activity of art criticism itself. While Lonzi *wrote* her questions before sending them to Twombly, in the later interviews, she freely formulated her questions during the conversations. But Twombly's presence/absence also brings up the question, evoked constantly throughout the conversations, of the crushing weight of American art. Actually, disapproval of American cultural hegemony is found in most of the book's voices. American artists embody the most recent trends where the sheer economic force behind the promotion their work imposes its laws on an art market that is already well on its way to becoming global. This clash can lead to bitter comments, like Fontana's, who, exasperated, states: "since we don't have the millions they do to launch our work, we are always an American sub-product" (p.92). Turcato, more nuanced in his considerations, sees "the invasion" of American art as the outcome of its ability "to amplify things in a way that here, in Europe, is totally unknown" (p.99). Likewise, Pascali compares the sense of action that is inherent, according to him, in American art and the contemplative nature of art that shackles European artists (pp. 92-93). American artists are seen in an ambivalent way as the people that must be challenged, often in the name of different causes like anti-capitalism or the defense of the European artistic tradition. For an analysis of anti-Americanism in the Italian art of the 1960s, in particular on the impact of the Vietnam War and the related protests, see Nicholas Cullinan, "From Vietnam to Fiat-nam. The Politics of Arte Povera," *October*, 124, Printemps, 2008, pp. 8–30. This attitude joins the widespread anti-Americanism in Italian cultural circles—many close to the Italian Communist Party and the radical left—with the desire of international success, a desire often tainted by the frustration and unhappiness with Italy's provincialism in the 1960s. These conversations testify to the power relations that color the international cultural politics at the time and Italy's subaltern role, torn between the promises of the American model and the rise of oppositional social movements the world over.

On the evolution of the perception of the United States in Italy during the 1960s, see Guido Crainz, *Il Paese mancato. Dal miracolo economico agli anni Ottanta*, Rome, Donzelli, pp. 121–132.

So, it's revealing that an important American artist like Twombly—one of the representatives of the New York School, symbol of American artistic supremacy—is present in the book as an absence. In reality, throughout his career, Twombly didn't lend himself to interviews: his refusal to answer Lonzi's questions was probably just a coincidence. Besides, most of the questions had been focused on the fact that he was one of the American artists who had been most influenced by European tradition. Including him in a book where the clash with American art is seen in a rather dramatic way could not be just a coincidence, especially if we remember that *Autoritratto* had been in large part assembled in the United States.

The second geographically offset actor is Salvatore Scarpitta, an Italian-American artist settled in New York that Carla Lonzi met during her American trip. By contrast, his interview, recorded in the U.S., gives a glimpse into the gap that separates him from his Italian counterparts, probably due to his geographical distance. Scarpitta isn't very interested in the controversies in the Italian artistic scene that take up a large part of *Autoritratto*'s conversations. He is clearly indifferent to the question of American cultural hegemony, and his societal worries are always conveyed through his work; he talks about his childhood, his art, and the techniques he adopts, often describing them in detail and with humor. This contrast jumps out at the reader: here, there is no trace of the tensions evoked above that are often the expression of a deep uneasiness with the strains that artists in Italy faced in the 1960s.

Unlike the Italian artists' shared view of American art, Italy seemed sluggish to them, still dominated by academic art, institutions that wouldn't support innovative artistic forms and the power, judged excessive, of art critics. The particular relation that Lonzi establishes with these artists ends up leaving free reign to openly criticize Italian art critics. The artist's words ring with the radical questioning of what Lonzi was actually doing—art criticism. Critics are accused of feeling "their hyperbolic... eh, their hyperbolic separation from artistic activity" (Fabro, p. 23), of only seeing what they wanted to on the canvas "and never what the paintings are" (Kounellis, p. 23), or of being "people who come and remain at the threshold" (Consagra, p. 199), and Lonzi even says art criticism is a "fake profession, completely fake" (p. 33), based on a power relation that makes the bond between the artist and society completely artificial.

Yet, despite the repeated attacks on Italian institutions, artists, and critics accused of complicity with power, the comments in *Autoritratto* can't really articulate a unique view concerning the political and social conflicts of the time. From this viewpoint, the discussions about the 1968 social movements show the artists' trouble grasping the new prospects for rethinking the power relations at the heart of the art world created by these revolts. Adopting the protest's logic meant running the risk of losing the idea of artistic freedom that the artists in *Autoritratto* didn't want to give up, insofar as it described art as an autonomous sphere, disinterested and outside of the social and political problems of the moment. This is why *Autoritratto* often gives us the impression that artists are thinking about events they aren't really participating in. The generation gap that separates them from the generation of '68 was probably to blame for that distance and for their bewilderment—that is, incomprehension, in seeing students protest against artistic institutions. Lonzi wrote a text against the 1968 Biennale di Venezia protest movement where she defended the artist's ability "to not identify with social structures" in the measure in which "artistic work [...] has a liberating capacity." For Lonzi, the Biennale di Venezia wasn't a reactionary place because it contained its own contradiction: "since it welcomes artists, it welcomes revolutionaries." So, while Lonzi considered artists as an intrinsically revolutionary category—and art as a critical activity in and of itself—she refused to see them as a socio-professional category. The artist, she insists in the conclusion of her text, is a marginal figure, "like an intellectual specialized in technical operations and, for this reason, not very accessible." In the same way, her defense of the Biennale didn't stop her from criticizing its role as an institution. However, her text here doesn't fully develop this critique, which saw an internal dialectic within artwork. See Carla Lonzi, "Biennale di Venezia e contestazione." In *Scritti sull'arte,* op. cit., pp. 558—560 (the article originally appeared in *L'Approdo Letterario* XIV, n. 44, October—December 1968, pp. 144—146) [our translation]. Here, the failed reading of the text written by Lonzi and Fabro (later cosigned by Paolini) during the occupation of the Triennale di Milano is suggestive. This text is integrally included in the pages of *Autoritratto,* p. 176.

Feminism will supply Carla Lonzi with a critical vocabulary able to propel her to the heart of the social, cultural, and political experiences of her time. However, her distance from the '68 revolts will never be disavowed, on the contrary: she will later claim that the feminist movement owed nothing to the 1968 protests, asserting its autonomy and its radicalness in respect to the oppositional movements of that period. On the complex relations between the birth of the feminist movement in Italy and the events of 1968, see Maria Luisa Boccia, *L'Io in Rivolta. Vissuto e pensiero di Carla Lonzi,* Milano, La Tartaruga, 1990, pp. 94—99 In this regard, it is interesting to remark that, in the pages of *Autoritratto,* Lonzi is suspicious of students, whom she describes as politicized and therefore insufficiently "creative" (p. 123), already old "in the head" (p. 214), while she is attracted by hippies, youth who refuse bourgeois conventions in favor of libertarian lifestyles. Unlike students, hippies don't want to transform society but rather concentrate on transforming the self: they focus on the experience of subjective change and don't try to write themselves into history. This figure of American import provides a kind of liberation based on subjective transformation, something much more interesting to Lonzi's eyes than the models embodied by the students who were bent on changing social structures from the outside. Transforming the world starting from the self: it is no coincidence that hippies reappeared in *"Sputiamo su Hegel,"* yet again in opposition to the politicized student, candidate for the role of oppressor. Carla Lonzi, *Sputiamo su Hegel,* op. cit., p. 33. The clash between hippies and students was also evident in the transgression of sexual roles: the hippies, writes Lonzi, experiment with non-patriarchal lifestyles that refused to separate the public and private. Idem, pp. 33–34. They gave body and voice to a gender blur that transformed their lives by mixing feminine and masculine.

The encumbering presence of the United States throughout the conversations is also a sign of the times when the book was assembled, between 1968 and 1969. These are two hinge years in Lonzi's own path, when she was moving away from art and, at the same time, awakening her feminist consciousness. These years include the 1968 events and the beginnings of an international feminist movement: toward the end of the 1960s, the first texts from American feminism began circulating in Italy along with the practice of *consciousness raising,* something Lonzi would adopt shortly thereafter in her *Rivolta Femminile* collective. On the circulation of American feminist texts in Italy, in particular see Luisa Passerini, "Corpi e corpo collettivo." In Teresa Bertilotti and Anna Scattigno (dir.), *Il femminismo degli anni Settanta*, Rome, Viella, 2005, pp. 181–193. On Carla Lonzi and the beginnings of Italian feminism, see M. L. Boccia, *L'Io in rivolta,* op. cit., pp. 67–104. Although information concerning her American experience is still quite patchy, there is no trace whatsoever of any contact with North American feminist groups in her diary. Lonzi was probably too busy transcribing *Autoritratto* and then, toward the end of her stay, occupied with her thyroid cancer that she would treat in a Boston hospital.

In the pages of the book, it is Carla Accardi who starts to ask about women's rights. Suggestively, she associates women's conditions with racism through numerous references to the civil rights struggles of African Americans. In particular, Accardi declares: "Yeah, what really interests me is the problem of the other, the other in respect to the white male. Who is the other in respect to the white male? Women... [...] Or either sex or race. Race, for example, the Blacks... They say: 'why do Blacks interest you?' I let the Blacks be because, as you can imagine, I have nothing to do with them as a white woman, but that's the thing that most interests me, you see? Because I feel closer to their side, the side of the other" (p. 118). The analogy between women and African Americans or the colonized, united under the banner of alterity, will be brought up in some of Lonzi's feminist writings at the beginning of the 1970s before disappearing, almost completely, from the key theories of Italian feminism. Italian feminism had a historical tendency to ignore questions on cultural and racial difference in favor of focusing on gender differences. See Vincenza Perilli, "Sexe et race dans les féminismes italiens. Jalons d'une généalogie," Cahiers du CEDREF, 14 / 2006. In the Italy of the 1960s still split by class struggles, experiencing massive migration from the rural south to an industrialized north, and absolutely unprepared to address its colonial past, the question of racism and cultural alterity could only be posed *via* the American Civil Rights Movement. The echo of the anticolonial struggles of the 1960s is in fact much more faint than those of African American struggles, showing to what extent the gaze of the artists—probably similar to those of Italian society as a whole—was turned towards the events on the other side of the pond.

It is hard to know how aware Lonzi was of the texts and debates in American feminism at that precise moment, specifically concerning the crossover of feminist and African American struggles. We do know that the parts where Accardi repeatedly comes back to the issue are from her second interview that, in all likelihood, overlaps with their decision to found a feminist collective, a decision that can be read between the book's last lines: "But I don't want to put it, now... I want there to be this man-woman problem, that's it. One day, someone says to me: 'that problem doesn't really exist.' No, no, no... the next morning, I get up and the problem exists" (p. 300).

RECORDING, MONTAGE, ARCHIVE

The tension all along the pages echoes the conflict that pits Carla Lonzi against art criticism and that takes up much of her attention. The tape recorder is the tool she chooses for undoing and, at the same time, reinventing art criticism. She goes back over this choice throughout the book, explaining her search for a form of writing that will allow the act of writing and the sound of her voice to coexist: "What attracts me personally to recording? Really what attracts me is something simple: it's being able to move from sounds to punctuation, to a text, it's finding a page that is not a written page but a page that... It's just like a chemical process, when condensation is produced... to know that a sound condenses into a sign, that's it, like gas passing to the liquid state" (p. 29).

An image goes along with this statement: Lonzi is sitting at a table, writing, with a pen, in front of a tape player. This photograph was taken in Minneapolis: with an air of concentration, Lonzi is confronted by the tape recorder's imposing presence. This image dialogues with the one on the left page, showing Scarpitta in his studio-garage full of racing cars; the artist, wearing a helmet, is posing passively on the side. These two images, which refer back to portions of the text where the artist talks about his automobile art and Lonzi about recording, put the subject in relation to machines. Scarpitta observes his automobiles, his hands resting on his knees, while the helmet, indicating his artist-pilot status, contrasts with his passive posture. Instead, on the right-hand page, Lonzi interacts with a tool where sounds and writing, body and automatism, are interwoven. The transcription of the artists' words means resorting to mechanical techniques since the sound is recorded and then replayed (reproduced) before becoming writing: this is the process Lonzi describes when she talks about "a sound [that] condenses into a sign" (*infra*).

In this sequence that suggests a kind of automatic writing, Lonzi writes by hand. She struggles through this new way of writing with audio recording from the idea that the mechanical reproduction of sound changes the very process of writing. As Friedrich Kittler has shown, the hegemony of writing had become seriously threatened near the end of the 19th century by new forms of media that offered alternative forms of communication destined to deeply affect writing itself. Friedrich Kittler, *Gramophone, Film, Typewriter*, Stanford, Stanford University Press, 1999. Audio recording ends up influencing written words and their retransmission/interpretation, especially in new practices that emphasize listening. For example, psychoanalysts record and transcribe the words of their patients. In this regard, see the entry dedicated to "Freud comme phonographe et écrivain." In F. Kittler, *Aufschreibesysteme. 1800-1900*, München, Wilhelm Fink, 1985, pp. 344–348. In the same way, Lonzi's work outlines a kind of mimesis with the machine: the artist's words are captured by the tape recorder and then retransmitted through writing in an informational flow that connects voice, machine, and the writer's hand. From this standpoint, Lonzi reinvents, through technique, the figure of the female writer/art critic as a medium of the artist's words. Lonzi's role is like the surrealist myth of woman as medium, sometimes saddled with a typewriter—like Man Ray's celebrated 1924 photograph portraying Simone Breton surrounded by the surrealist group Man Ray, *Séance de rêve éveillé*, 1924, b&w photograph.—since she listens and transcribes predominantly male words. However, what Lonzi is doing is fundamentally different: she is not only actively participating in the conversations—transcribing her own voice as well—but she is also piloting the entire endeavor into a specific kind of montage-writing.

Lonzi began recording the interviews for the review *Marcatré*, directed by Eugenio Battisti.

Marcatré is one of the main Italian avant-garde reviews of the 1960s; it was close to Gruppo 33 and founded in Genoa in 1963 by the historian and art critic Eugenio Battisti. This review included musicians, art historians, architects, writers, and art critics on its editorial board, with members such as Gillo Dorfles, Edoardo Sanguineti, Umberto Eco, Paolo Portoghesi, Silvano Bussotti, and Vittorio Gregotti. A young Germano Celant was the editorial secretary. Eugenio Battisti (1924–1989) is the author of landmark monographs on Giotto and Brunelleschi, and his book *L'Antirinascimento* [The Anti-Renaissance] (1962) laid the foundations for an inventive reinterpretation of Mannerism. In 1963 he founded the *Museo sperimentale d'arte contemporanea* [The Experimental Museum of Contemporary Art] in Genoa, and the *Marcatré* review was published until 1970. He was also a pioneer of industrial archeology in Italy. On Lonzi and the *Marcatré* review, see L. Iamurri, "Carla Lonzi e il *Marcatré*." In Carla Lonzi, *Scritti sull'arte,* op. cit., pp. 707–723. Carla Lonzi was a marginal presence in this review, which was wholly dedicated to contemporary culture and intellectual experimentation, far from the conservative spirit that animated *L'Approdo* and Roberto Longhi's teachings. In the pages of this heterodox review, Lonzi began to experiment with forms of critical writing that differed from her previous experiences. As Laura Iamurri underscores, the approaches to knowledge expressed in that review were probably a chief source of inspiration for her, in particular the ethnographic studies that relied on use of tape recorders. The *Marcatré* review included a section entitled Class Culture and Contemporary Folklore in which it published, in the 1965 summer issue, the transcription of interviews and the montage of different sources realized in a militant ethnographic perspective. It is in the following issue, notes Iamurri, that Lonzi's first interview (with Luciano Fabro) appears. L. Iamurri, "Intorno a Autoritratto.

Fonti, ipotesi, riflessioni." In L. Conte et al. (dir.), *Carla Lonzi: la duplice radicalità*, op. cit., pp. 75–80. So, the "Discorsi" [Discourses] section that Lonzi introduced into the pages of *Marcatré* in 1966 was part of a transdisciplinary framework and gave rise to "a new strategy of active presence, Laura Iamurri, "Carla Lonzi sul 'Marcatré'," op. cit., p. 715 [our translation]." a way of placing artists on the side as a way to make their experience subjective. Lonzi's work with these completely opposite reviews wasn't only a rupture: the choice of audio recording as a medium for writing conjures the fact that *L'Approdo* was, above all, a radio program. The texts written for that review had to satisfy the needs of both written publication as well as of audio broadcasting. Reading and listening are two connected but distinct activities, and it may be in the balance between these two ways of communicating that Lonzi's interest for the spoken word, sound, and their possible written translation began to develop.

Autoritratto is not a simple transcript of interviews because Lonzi cuts the continuum of the dialogues and recomposes it, putting a series of images taken from private archives together with the text. Resorting to montage for composing the book seems almost to be a logical outcome of her use of the tape recorder: formatting recorded audio material meant stepping back and then recomposing the conversation. This process of montage makes the images scattered throughout the book dialogue with the text without ever illustrating it. In fact, the images draw all their meaning from the dynamic that their presence spurs in the reader and the stunning relations between different images and between image and text. As Georges Didi-Huberman writes, montage is not merely a formal procedure but also a way of producing knowledge that means distancing yourself from the material and, consequently, taking a stance. Georges Didi-Hubermann, *Quand les images prennent position. L'œil de l'histoire 1*, Paris, Minuit, 2009. For Lonzi, arranging texts and images means disorganizing their normal sequence in order to create a fragmented unity and, at the same time, showing the reader the incomplete nature of what they are reading. Montage, again highlights Didi-Huberman, is a new arrangement of things starting from their differences, an act that renders everything foreign, unusual, as if we saw these things for the first time. Ivi, pp. 69–73.

The book's photographs were most often supplied by the artists themselves: alongside the twenty-some reproductions of artworks are photographs of the artists and Carla Lonzi in their daily lives, in the studio, on social occasions, or at expositions, accompanied by family photos of childhood memories or family vacations. In all, it creates an ensemble where different time periods are superimposed. The intimate charm of these images lends itself to the swirl of relations and affects that are wrapped up around Carla Lonzi. So, the book has a spatial dimension that is both moving and incomplete since it isn't a systematic knowledge base of the artists in the book but a subjective implication in that knowledge, which supposes emotion, affect, and conflict. In this sense, it can be read as the attempt to undo a narration of art history focused on a model of linear time and on supposed neutrality, coming much closer to an art history, still uncommon at the time, more interested

in art as the mediation between history and subjectivity. Griselda Pollock, *Encounters in the Virtual Feminist Museum, op.cit.*, p. 12.

Autoritratto outlines an incomplete history of a lived
present in the first person. In this framework, the agency of the images in the textual space that, at first glance
recalls the role of illustrations in art history textbooks,
allows a multiplicity of often dissonant and always fragmentary narrations to emerge. We might say the book
depicts this approach to knowledge as an imaginary
museum redesigned based on a subjective space. An
intimate diary, Lonzi transcribes a lived and imag(in)
ed experience in this volume in a process where a specifically feminine form of writing becomes a new way
to create knowledge rooted in introspection and auto-
biography. Producing knowledge from subjective experience is a distinctive trait of feminist practices, particularly in the 1960s-1970s: it is no coincidence that,
a few years later, Lonzi would specifically choose diary
writing for its feminist potential. Regarding the analogies
between intimate diaries, maps, atlases and archives, see
Giuliana Bruno's pages dedicated to Gerhard Richter's *Atlas* in
Giuliana Bruno, *Atlas of Emotion. Journeys into Art, Architecture,
and Film*, London, Verso, 2002, pp. 331–357. Choosing photographs and assembling them with the texts thus helps
form this subjective and feminine space. It makes a
"room of one's own," and *Autoritratto* makes that room
visible and readable.

FORTY-SIX THOUGHTS ON RADIO
Kenneth Goldsmith

The beauty of radio is its off-switch. No matter what comes across the airwaves—no matter how annoying, absurd, or incongruous—you can always turn it off. The off-switch is a tool of empowerment for both broadcaster and listener. It allows the broadcaster to take chances, and it allows the listener to opt-out.

Sitting alone in a studio broadcasting to 10,000 people, one must maintain the illusion that no one is listening.

You can never know exactly to whom you're broadcasting, so it is useless trying to pander to an audience. At the same moment, one listener may be manacled at work, while another may be manacled to a bedpost.

There are certain ruts and habits a DJ gets into. Automatic segues. Automatic segues. One tends to repeat these again and again. The secret: the audience never notices.

Radio is background, not foreground. You are always doing something while listening—with one ear—to the radio. Nobody sits by the radio and just listens—with the exception of people driving. Along with artists, drivers are the best listeners. Artists' hands and eyes are busy, but their ears are wide open. As a result, visual artists know more about music than anyone else on the planet.

When I first began broadcasting, I tried to make perfect segues from other people's music. When I became good at that, presenting other people's music became tedious. So I began to sing on the radio. I have a lousy voice. I would sing in front of generic karaoke tracks, enhancing my voice with the studio tools. Soon, I began putting on long instrumental tracks like John Coltrane's "My Favorite Things" and singing Roland Barthes texts on top of them. I would do this sometimes for three hours at a time. Of course, it drove the listeners crazy.

Bertolt Brecht said, "I wish that they would graft an additional device onto the radio—one that would make it possible to record and archive for all time, everything that can be communicated by radio. Later generations would then have the chance of seeing with amazement how an entire population—by making it possible to say what they had to say to the whole world—simultaneously made it possible for the whole world to see that they had absolutely nothing to say."

When I first got on the air at WFMU, the hippest radio station in the world, I took the on-air name Kenny G, which is, in fact, my real name. It drove the listeners crazy at first, but over time, I became their Kenny G as opposed to the sax player.

When I first arrived at the station in 1995, I set up a primitive homepage that said

"Welcome to Kenny G's homepage" with a link to email me. It being the early days of the web, many people thought that they had found the "real" Kenny G's secret homepage, made even more convincing by the fact that it was hosted by a radio station. I soon began getting fan mail intended for the sax-playing Kenny G, lots of it. I never wrote the fans back, fearing that word would get out that I was not him and then the emails would stop. Each week, I would take the strangest, most obsessive letters and read them aloud on my show as if they were addressed to me. My bed music was always the Kenny G Christmas record.

One evening in an Italian restaurant in Chelsea, I got up to go to the bathroom. On the way, I overheard two traditionally dressed gentlemen mention the name "Kenny G." Tispy as I was, I marched right up to the table and said, "Did I hear you say the name Kenny G? Well, I'm Kenny G!" They looked at me askance. I repeated my statement: "I'm Kenny G." One of the gentlemen said, "Nice to meet you, but I'm Kenny G's agent." And it was true. This guy was the other Kenny G's agent. I told him about my radio show and asked if it was possible for Kenny G to be on the Kenny G show. He smiled, said "Of course!" and I gave him my business card. We shook hands, and he said he'd call me. I never heard from him again.

In 2003, I was on the radio Thursday evenings from 8—11pm. It just so happened that just as I went on the air on Thursday, March 20, 2003, the deadline for Saddam Hussein to leave Iraq had passed. For the next two hours, the country— and the world—was on edge, knowing that we were on the brink of war. It was just a matter of time until the invasion was to begin. I knew I couldn't do a normal show, so instead, from 8pm on, I played only eerie recordings of shortwave numbers stations, mostly created during the cold war, which were numbers repeated amidst bursts of feedback, static, and odd electronic sounds. At 10pm, we invaded Iraq. I continued to play these numbers stations but had my computer read out, in computer voice, short announcements like "The invasion has begun" and "We will destroy the enemy." I never spoke—and so it went on for three hours, a creepy hazy ambiance, which I thought was the only way to mark such an event.

The World Trade Center attacks happened right across the river from the WFMU studio. They occurred on a Tuesday; I went on the air that Thursday. During my shift, I played Allen Ginsberg's "Kaddish" in its entirety and Gorecki's "Symphony No. 3: Sorrowful Songs." I didn't speak on the show.

I was on the air on the morning after Obama was elected, from 9am to noon. I played Parliament's 1976 five-minute long "Chocolate City" over and over again for an entire three hours without interruption.

Each week, I had three hours to kill. That's the way I saw it. How to fill up three hours?

In 2007, J.K. Rowling released the seventh and final *Harry Potter and the Deathly Hallows*. Prior to the book's release the day I went on the air, someone had leaked a copy to the Internet, enraging Scholastic Books, who threatened anybody distributing it with a heavy lawsuit. I printed out and sang in my horrible voice the very last chapter of the book on the air, thereby spoiling the finale of the series for anyone listening. During my show, the station received an angry call from Scholastic Books. It appears that their whole office was listening to WFMU that afternoon. Nothing ever came of it.

In the mid-90s, it was made illegal to distribute the DECSS code that was used to crack DVDs for replication. With this in mind, I read the entire code over the air and played songs that used the code as lyrics. I faked my arrest on air, leaving my shift a half-hour early, the air dead, the studio empty.

When I began doing radio, I was told by the station manager that my on-air voice was too smooth, too professional sounding. He suggested that I add some "ums" and "uhs" during my mic breaks to sound more like an average person.

On the air, not having anything to say, I began reading blogs that had nothing to do with me. For one show I'd read from blogs written by obese people trying desperately to lose weight. Another, I'd read from anorexic blogs written by skeletal people trying to gain weight. The following week, I'd read from depressive people trying to get happy. Because radio is not a visual medium, people had no idea what I really looked liked. And because I read so convincingly so as to sound like I was talking naturally, listeners thought I was, one week, wildly overweight or terribly emaciated the next. They had no idea that I was an average man, of average size and average weight.

Radio is best heard, not seen. Whenever you see an image of your favorite radio personality, you are inevitably disappointed.

One week, Gregory Whitehead came on my show, and we had people call in and scream as loudly as they could for three hours.

My show was technologically determined. There was a time when, in the finder window, you could play several MP3s simultaneously, each with their own volume control and each able to be fast-forwarded and reversed. In essence, the computer's finder became a mixer. But then Apple changed their OS and deleted that feature. When that happened, I was no longer able to do my show the way I used to. It led to the end of my involvement in radio.

With Vicki Bennett, we did a show for three hours where we were bound to each other and gagged. We kept the mics on the entire time. Each half-hour, one rope was cut. The show started out silent. By the end, it was full-on noise.

For three hours, I whispered the entirety of Karl Marx's *Communist Manifesto* whilst dressed in an expensive suit.

I played for three hours, a tape of two men sleeping. The silence was punctured by snores.

For three hours I played the sounds of farts.

It is said that a baby's cry is the most attention-getting sound in the human catalog of sounds. I once looped a piercing baby's cry for an hour.

At first, listeners would call and complain. But after a decade or so, the complaints stopped. Those who didn't wish to listen, left. The rest learned to either listen or else tolerate my weekly intrusion.

My show started off being called "Unpopular Music," so you knew what you were getting into beforehand. If there were complaints, I would say, you were warned.

My idea was to get the listener to turn the radio off. When you challenge someone not to listen, they listen harder.

My initial inspiration: the Mothers of Invention's *Absolutely Free*, a collage which fused pop, noise, sound poetry, and classical music.

For a short time, the FCC allowed us to say swear words on air. I seem to recall that you could say them ten minutes apart and that you were allowed to use them in a political way ("The government is fucked") but not in a sexual way ("I want to fuck Laura Bush"). This lasted for a month or two and was then predictably rescinded.

My own work was informed by my years in radio. I learned how to speak publically and consciously. I learned how to lie convincingly. I learned how the pitch and timbre of the voice can juice a situation.

For weeks, I would play the sources for my books on the air. For instance, for three weeks straight, I broadcast nothing but 1010 WINS traffic reports, which came to be my book *Traffic*. Then for the three weeks following that, I would read live on the air, my transcripts of those traffic reports. That killed six weeks, 18 hours. I did the same for weather reports and baseball games.

I had the idea to bring a radio into the studio and simply rebroadcast another station for three hours. I would just pull the mic down to the radio and walk away. I was told that this was highly illegal.

As long as you didn't violate FCC codes, you could do anything you like for three hours. I always wondered why DJs would bother to play it safe when they were given all the freedom in the world. Why would they bother to pander to an audience, to be loved? (We weren't paid, so it couldn't have been about money or ratings.)

"Every once in a while," said station manager Ken Freedman when fending off listener complaints about my show, "you're just going to have to turn your radio off."

Oftentimes I would back-announce song titles for songs I didn't play.

Other times, I would back-announce song titles from another DJ's sets and shows for the entire three hours. Nobody seemed to notice.

I would transcribe my fellow DJs mic breaks and then read them as my own during my show. Nobody seemed to notice.

During a fundraiser once, I played musical sets from a popular rock 'n' roll DJ's show and faithfully backannounced them as my own. I didn't raise any more money than I normally did.

In the end, each week on the air was three hours of performance art. I couldn't keep that up forever.

I organized sets by keyword. Pick a topic, say, "dog," and search an MP3 library containing hundreds of thousands of files for ID3 tags that had "dog" in them (which, naturally, had "god" in it). I'd come up with a beautiful freeform set, not based on how songs sound, but by what they're about. The more MP3s in the collection, the richer the possibilities became. Oftentimes, I never heard the song I was to play in the set, but because it had a keyword I was looking for, it conceptually worked.

iTunes allows you to sort songs according to their length. One week, I programmed three hours of audio that was all under thirty seconds long. The next week, I repeated the concept, this time with songs lasting exactly one minute.

When I ran out of ideas for a new show, I would just play one of my old shows in the public MP3 archive. Nobody ever knew the difference.

It was a delight to do back-to-back shows with Irwin Chusid—for years people have said that they thought we were the same person because our voices are almost identical. Many weeks, we switched and pretended we were the other DJ. The listenership couldn't tell the difference.

Why, in this age, when everybody can download all the MP3s they want from the web, do we still listen to radio? Because we need someone to make sense of it all, someone with a sensibility to put it together for us, someone to narrate this mass of information.

ACOUSTIC PROMISES FOR THE FUTURE
Francesco Bernardelli

If a general consensus can be granted to the notion that in recent decades a significant increase took place in the sensibility towards a broader cultural reception of expanded modes of communication—as substantiated through the ample potentialities of sound experiments, new auditive configurations, and radio waves' actual possibilities—this phenomenon should be related to the gradual change of the sonic dimension itself, the (so-called) "aural" aspect, closely connected to a perceptual redefinition of the basic fundaments of the cultural producer/audience-relationship.

Such a sort of "aural/auditory boom," which first manifested itself throughout a minimal set of possibilities and then gradually acquired more and more basic but relevant features, has to be considered closely linked to the new growing technologies that were flourishing in parallel at that time. The frame of reference cannot be restricted to the technologies of sound-making and sound-transmitting alone. When making and experiencing sound(s) through an increasingly complex technical apparatus began to appear and circulate, wider cultural issues and newer concepts of communication arose, equally relevant and central to a better focused understanding of the whole issue (of communication media), and ultimately related to the political and ideological uses of the radio device.

With time and the rapidly increasing transformation of the nature of radio broadcast, a different visibility and significance of the presence of radio devices, as manifested through the wide set of choices offered by updated forms of telecommunication first and later by the Internet (an ever-increasing specialization of web radio channels, the possibilities to register with personalized podcasts, and so on...), seem to have resulted in an expansion of the historically framed interpretation of the transmitter/receiver-issue. Such continuously evolving transformation has also enhanced not only the direct relation between producers and listeners but also the very customization of the actual communicative experience to the degree that couldn't be foreseen twenty, even ten years ago.

In the wake of this phenomenon, looking more precisely at the relationship between the vast area of communication media and sound(s) as a material of production on the one hand, and the field of acoustic experiments (anticipating what later turned to be recognized as Sound Art—something which emerged in the 60s) on the other hand, what starts to appear is a drastic readjustment of all the possible interactions. The manifold questions surrounding issues of spatiality, contiguity, and accessibility in the sound arts' as well as in the related visual arts' domain that already began to gain a certain importance during their appearance in the late '60s/early '70s "intermedia" installations, were offered and increasingly situated on the basis of the experimental sounds' properties.

We cannot overlook the conceptual importance of innovative experiences like John Cage's trajectory and ideas (think just of works like "Imaginary land-scapes")—or the many, sometimes almost forgotten, innovative experiences that the official radio field brought up and put forward... from the specific reper-tory of Radio theater (more or less experimental), as well as specific Library Music collections or the vast new Music Theatre's arena of proposals, provocations, and debates—until now a very relevant and refined new field open for reflection and discussion, although marked sometimes by an almost too academic approach in analyzing/criticizing specific idiosyncratic experi-ences and critical contexts.

Art and radio have had perhaps the most unexpected kind of relationship among the already long trajectory of twentieth-century modern arts. It is difficult not to think of the rich documentation per-taining to the historical avant-garde's heroic times—as manifested by Marinetti's (and Giuseppe Masna-ta's) manifesto *La Radia* (1933) or Bertolt Brecht's writings (*The Radio as an Apparatus of Communication*, 1932) on the utopian potentialities of radio broadcast-ing, a technology already able to switch "from distri-bution to communication"—not just a receiving de-vice but also something able to transmit information—we cannot but recall the vital connections that have run deeply in between these aforementioned disciplinary fields, maintaining not only technically and artistical-ly but also aesthetically significant qualities that have been absorbed and subsumed by a broader landscape of users (beyond the initial much more artistic and activist group of users).   Suffice it to say that after the Second World War, North American and European culture started to be informed (if not entirely dominated) by the ubiquitous presence of mainstream media culture—cinema, radio, and television, not to mention new advertising techniques—quickly leading to an increasingly saturated "mediascape" (as we would call it nowadays). Where cinema and television could profit from the enjoyment offered by movement and visibility, radio opted for a different role, private, almost intimate, directed at touching the invisible threads of the public's emotional lives.   While during the earlier times of radio, the core-content seemed to contain and deliver quite a significant amount of speech-based programs, after the inception of television (as the main form of electronic entertainment and information), radio formats and schedules became increasingly dominated by various offers of music programming.

If the reality of mass media seemed to increasingly become society's reality—everything we know about the world and society comes filtered from the mass media complex—the people's perception of everyday life appeared to be shaped by mass media, and subsequently most of society started to adopt behavioral patterns generated by mass media which still tended to represent a not-necessarily consensual reality.

One of the major problems connected to Radio's expansive practices, as we may imagine, is how it was derived from military-related research and development, primarily conceived as tools of social control. Such military-industrial flourishing of the radio apparatus itself offered every audience a particular challenge: how to cross over the still-prevailing influences of those initial sources and how to be able to imagine a new platform for application regarding ideas—not to be immediately absorbed and transformed by the dominant power structures. Marinetti and Masnata had already declared that Radio was still too keen in maintaining a subsidiary relation to music ("istupidita da musica"—dumbed down by music—was the definition), so it could be argued that in the new developing concepts of state-of-the-art (avant-garde) radio stations, in the UK and in the USA as early as the early/mid-twenties, such a notion (of a traditional, direct relation to music-broadcasting) was challenged by radical options/new forms of expression as manifested through highly original and unique sound concept and design practices. A new generation of tech-wise entertainers and engineers had entered the game. A great deal of description and writing has been devoted to the pioneering endeavors of figures who adopted and perfected narrative techniques like Orson Welles (with his memorable *The War of the Worlds*' broadcast experiment in 1939), which literally seem to sum up the actual turning point represented by the technical possibilities' advancements by the fourth decade of the twentieth century.

If we take a look from a broader perspective, then—since the mid-sixties—during a time of self-perceived rapid and radical social change (like both the sixties and seventies decades seemed to channel and foster), a rapidly spreading interest—if not a true need for alternative sources of music, entertainment, and information, motivated by the desire of finding mass-media closer to the youngsters' sphere of interests rather distant and different from the State-controlled network of broadcasting radios, materialized in the activities of so-called pirate (clandestine) UK radio stations (Radio Caroline, Radio Veronica, Radio London, etc.), turning out to be the antithesis of the typical BBC-style and their monopoly.

Innovative concepts of communication, participation, and interaction—moving from receptive to active involvement—have long been key questions to progressive artists, especially after the Second World War. New works—better operative systems concerning artists and recipients—had been implying a (conceptual) movement from the "closed" to the "open" idea of a work of art, from the static object to the dynamic process, from pure contemplative reception to mediated and/or active participation.   While in the 1960s the media conglomerate was considered as one of several adoptable means in order to urge the socio-cultural utopia of a society under transformation, a further turning moment took place in the 90s, a situation in which media technology entered another phase through the rise of the Internet, a major paradigmatic shift re-establishing a new significance of the notions of social interaction and interactivity, which now increasingly describe media-assisted human exchange and therefore link up with the ideals of the 1960s intermedia art as well as the 1970s and 1980s early telecommunications experiments. The electronic space (a virtual plus real space) proved to become a sort of "communication sculpture" where social networking systems, communication platforms, and new digital entities fostered participation; collective and collaborative telecommunication projects shifted from the heavy and large analog media of the late 1980s to the small digital media of the 1990s: new spatial and network interconnections paved the way to open text(s), open theories, and ultimately open and participatory co-writing and co-authoring projects on the web. But this is a most recent history.

As has been remarked since the end of seventies by journalists and sociologists, "in highly complex societies like ours, which function through a finely graded system of divided (i.e. specialized) labour, the crucial question has to do with which specific ideologies, representing the interests of which specific groups and classes will prevail at any given moment, in any given situation" Richard "Dick" Hebdige, *Subculture*, 1979, p.14. The extraordinary growth of free radios originated such a strong reaction that, because of the popularity of pirate radios, already in 1967 BBC radio was restructured, establishing BBC Radio 1, Radio 2, Radio 3, and Radio 4. A good number of DJs of the newly created pop music service subsequently came from pirate stations.

Trying to reconnect with such juvenile requests, national broadcast programs were established—both in the UK (BBC had introduced programs like *Ready Steady Go!* and *Saturday Club*) and in Italy (*Bandiera Gialla, Alto gradimento, Per voi giovani, Supersonic...*). Almost inevitably, reference models became outdated quickly, no longer in tune with a rapidly shifting society that was increasingly accelerating demands for more and more openness, and not just related to the music sphere. In the case of Italy, some foreign broadcasting companies—Radio Montecarlo (on the western coastal side) and Radio Capodistria (on the eastern side) proved to be highly innovative and influential, drastically changing the parameters of the way such broadcasts used to be conducted. A whole new outlook, much more informal and fresh and quite distant from the rigid attitude that had marked the history of the radio quickly took off. The relevance of the rapidly developed consequences (in the speaking codes of adopted jargon, ways of saying, etc.) clearly manifested how signifying practices as represented through a viable identifying device—widespread as the radio—could hit huge sectors of society in just about few months or even weeks.

Precisely after the large turmoils of 1968 and '69 (and the related following seasons), in Italy new conditions seemed to appear as expressed by the desire and the demands of large sectors of society expressing their wishes to be able to freely choose different sources of information (counter-information as it happened to be defined) quite distant from the mainstream media. The historical precedents of American and English broadcasters, inclusive of nearly legendary pirate radios, characterized by a "different" style and a unique mixture of music and words, offered some different experiences, actually proposing to overcome the monopoly of State-owned Radio Rai. The new technological push, although rather primitive and "poor," with the appearance of available transistor radios and the new F(requency) M(odulation) stereo, as well as the changing laws (especially the landmark ruling by the Constitutional Court in July 1976), encircled the boom of free radios, both private and local. From 1975 to 1980, many brand new radio stations managed to go "on the air," literally revolutionizing the political, social, and cultural Italian soundscape (and landscape). It was a peculiar and unique case—compared to the rest of Europe—for the quite daring and aggressive ways in which they arrived at the factual liberalization of the airwaves. A competitive pluralism and a mixed system were in fact imposed. Listening to such a quickly expanding horizon/network of radio activities helped form a true revolution of languages and communicative tools (and the whole way of approaching people and their needs). Brilliantly condensed by Federico Campagna: "*counter-information* had the potential of becoming a means to create new worlds, rather than to describe the existing one." Looking much more in detail at Italy, the turning point of 1974 into 1975 marks an important moment in the redefinition of the presence of radio broadcast: the region of Emilia Romagna, Bologna—on the 23rd of November, 1974—had RadioBologna (the full name being "per l'accesso pubblico," for public access) transmitting from a little white caravan on top of a nearby hill—colle dell'Osservanza—while another city, Parma, saw the appearance of the eponymous radio station, which started on the very first day of January 1975, and was soon followed by cities like Milan (Radio Milano International, Radio Milano Centrale) in March 1975, Rome (Radio Roma—June 1975, Radio Roma 103), Biella, and many others.

Within a few months, all the available frequencies in the context of larger cities were taken by a myriad of quickly established free radio stations, also with the inevitable consequence of many superimposed radio entities on the same bandwidth. The sheer variety of programs and activities covered a largely unmapped territory of new music and new tendencies (the full chart of daily broadcast was helped by the introduction/use of pre-recorded tapes) but, most important, a new direct contact between the public and the radio conductors with a stronger emphasis on audience participation sprung out. Open microphone and live/direct broadcast became a whole new ground, open to literally unheard possibilities that were pretty much in sync with those fast transformations that society had experienced in recent years. Basically, the live broadcasting activity originated from home-made studios.

Although since the early seventies, authorities like the Ministry of Post and Telecommunications claimed that pirate radio could cause interference with official (licensed) broadcasters and could interfere with frequencies used by emergency services, the new regulations introduced between 1975 (Law n° 103-14/04/1975) and 1976 by the Constitutional Court (it is important to remember the sentence n° 202/1976, 28/07/1976) tried to limit the widespread diffusion of this constantly enlarging number of players, underlying the regime of state monopoly regarding Radio and TV broadcast, but allowing cable transmission and "circularity"—a definition that helped in many ways (and in countless public trials) against the seizure of equipment. There was also an article from a pre-existing law (n° 848, 04/08/1955) about the *Protection of the Human Rights and Fundamental Freedoms*—an international treaty recognized in Italy—that helped the freedom of radio broadcasting. In the summer of 1976, the Constitutional Court offered a new interpretation on the subject and declared inadmissible with an historic judgment (n° 202 of July 28, 1976) the parts of the laws prohibiting broadcast in local areas: that sentence fostered the further expansion of the radio platform—the success was palpable with an even-larger number of new "free" radio and television stations immediately taking off.

A new era had begun; while major TV and radio stations played their game within the larger infrastructure of mainstream information channels, most of the pirate/free radio stations played a very significant role within a position circumscribed not by a constituted address or by a set up officialized status but imbued with a stronger and active attitude, which was in full transformative flux. To speak about some sort of social or professional order (the so-called "division of tasks and work") within the energy-bursting activity would simply be a misleading idea; no actual, explicit acts of labeling or defining ever came into being... it was always much more the case of a mutually acknowledged acceptance of being there, available, active and open, receptive, and against the typical bureaucratic tendencies to fix established (and ultimately hierarchical) roles. Although marked by an extreme inner fragility and volatility, the collective nature of such endeavors brought back a different sense of fulfillment and realization, although most of the working activities operated as self-regulating flexible systems where associates, colleagues, members, and friends preferred to keep working, choosing their roles based on their mutual affinities, curiosity, and willingness to keep a basic openness to very fundamental questions about roles, functions, and the final aim of all those incredible streams of activities. The result was certainly something much more "offered" (as a sort of Potlatch-like activity) than "taken"—or just absorbed—from the specific socio-cultural context in which they chose to work.

Nearly forty years later, it is rather difficult to think of radio stations as free broadcasting agents; it is much easier to view them as competitive commercial ventures. Unfortunately, their commercial needs, their format, and even organizational structure have somehow leveled to the most common musical\cultural tastes, largely dismissing any idea of experimentation—quite remote from the "time in which utopia was already happening." However, some strong and self-renovating energy has been spreading through the realm of new platforms, especially the web-radio network.

As pointed out already by Hebdige, "forms cannot be permanently normalized. They can always be deconstructed, demystified... moreover, commodities can be symbolically 'repossessed' in everyday life, and endowed with implicitly oppositional meanings, by the very groups who originally produced them." That actual re-appropriation, not just operative on a metaphorical level, but much more effectively on the daily basis of a powerful transformative ability, happened where (to quote Henri Lefebvre) "objects in practice become signs and signs objects and a second nature takes the place of the first—the initial layer of perceptible reality" Henri Lefebvre, *Everyday Life in the Modern World*, 1971, with the consequence that there have always been "objections and contradictions which hinder the closing of the circuit between sign and object, production and reproduction."

Exactly at the crossing between the renewed interest in the flexibility of medium and the persistence of previous disciplines' means and operative patterns, we rediscover the ample margins of a concrete utopia—maybe something closer to the spreading of a transformative virus. Given the fact that the very meaning of communication, most of the time, has to be accurately channeled (we all know that, properly speaking, communication begins if someone understands what someone else has given as an information), it is necessary to reflect on the fundamental properties of a medium: something invisible. Niklas Luhmann in *The Reality of Mass Media*, 2009 pointed out how we can only see and watch the form of media. Media have requirements for form and manifest and reproduce themselves through the construction of an articulation of forms. In order to (re)create a lively sense of perception—an experience/embodiment—we are somehow compelled to turn the listener into a sort of performer, a co-author. In that sense, the listener—by deliberately choosing his/her own side—has to take an active part (as soon as he/she enters) in the experience in fundamentally different ways than in live performance, and in order to fulfill such a task, it is necessary to recompose and put together several disparate elements into the music/audio-stream, elements that are non-linear, occasionally random and not discursive, sometimes even noisy and disturbing in a way like a lot of anti-traditional, radically experimental music. Here the interesting parallel with experimental sounds and sound art new territories seem to work.

The very idea of being able to challenge listeners anew at each and every hearing, in the Here & Now of the actual acoustic/listening experience, as practiced in the heydays of radical (libertarian) practices, is sought after in order to reach a place where even apparently identical sounds will end up sounding entirely different depending on the performance the listener creates in his own mind or ear— the essence of the sound. Acoustic experience doesn't lie as much in its details as in the act of trying to bring them together, link them and understand them.

ARTISTS' BOOKS FOR AIRPORT
Delphine Bedel

"One day I'd like to see artists' books ensconced in supermarkets, drugstores, and airports and, not incidentally, to see artists to be able to profit economically from broad communication rather than from the lack of it." (Lippard, 1977) Lucy Lippard, "The Artist's Books Goes Public," *Art in America*, January/February 1977.

WHAT IS A BOOK?

'What is a book?' Confronted with the illegal publishing of his books, Immanuel Kant writes in a short text defining a book in the *Metaphysics of Morals* "Why does unauthorised publishing, which strikes one even at first glance as unjust, still have an appearance of being rightful? Because on the one hand a book is a corporeal artifact (opus mechanicum) that can be reproduced (by someone in legitimate possession of a copy of it), so that there is a right to a thing with regard to it. On the other hand a book is also a mere discourse of the publisher to the public, which the publisher may not repeat publicly without having a mandate from the author to do so (praestatio operae), and this is a right against a person. The error consists in mistaking one of these rights for the other" (Immanuel Kant, "What Is a Book?" In *Metaphysics of Morals*, (31/II), 1792) Kant's definition was unusual for the time (Pozzo, 2006) Ricardo Pozzo, "Immanuel Kant sobre propriedade intelectual," *Trans/Form/Ação* (São Paulo), v.29(2), 2006, pp.11–18.. For him, the book is, on the one hand, the product of manufacturing that grants the buyer with ownership and, on the other, a discourse with an 'agency of rights.' His understanding of authors' rights received little attention at the time. Copyright came out of publishing in the 17th and 18th centuries. (Authors' rights as such did not exist in Germany at that time; the publisher or bookseller was granted the authorisation for the first print.) When publishing migrates from paper to pixel, is this duality still relevant? Is there a continuum or a revolution? Various historians, such as Roger Chartier, are reconsidering this legacy regarding contemporary issues of authorship, publishing, ownership, and readership "Le livre: son passé, son avenir, Entretien avec Roger Chartier" interview by Ivan Jablonka, *La Vie des Idées*, Paris, September 29, 2008..

STORIES BELONG TO EVERYONE

Until the 17th century, stories belonged to everyone; most books had no punctuation as they were meant as a collective experience to be 'read for the ear' before becoming to be 'read by the eye' in the intimate silence of a room. The 18th-century transformation defined the book and its layout as we now know it. Theater plays were often written as a collaborative process. They would not be published unless there was an outstanding success and publishers would select only one of the authors' names for the cover (Chartier, 2011). "In the age of the codex, a hierarchy of objects could more or less indicate a hierarchy in terms of validity of discourse." Ibidem. In a recent interview, Roger Chartier argues that with e-publishing comes the most significant break in the Kantian definition <u>Ibidem.</u>:

"So we have powerful reasons to assert that mobility of texts. There are others who are intellectual or aesthetic: to romance, the stories belong to everyone and texts are written using formulas already there. This malleability stories, this plurality of available resources for writing, creating another form of movement, impossible to lock in the letter of a text that would be stable forever."

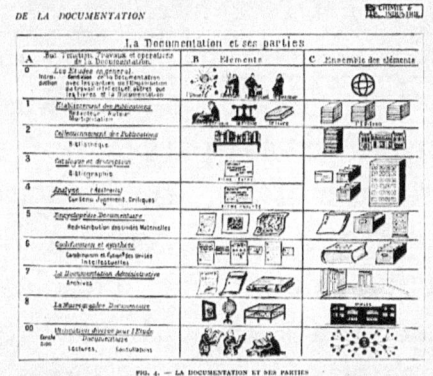

And one might add that the copyright only reinforces this fact. This is, of course, ironic since the copyright recognizes that the work is always identical to itself. But what does copyright protect? In the eighteenth and nineteenth centuries, it protects all possible forms of printed text and now all possible forms of publication of the text, whether a film adaptation, a TV program or multiple issues. There is, therefore, a principle of a legal unit that covers just the indefinite plurality of successive or simultaneous statements of the work.

As major retail companies like Amazon take the opportunity and are in fact becoming "publishers," it is remarkable that artists' publishing activities have not yet taken this digital turn. As the U.S. publisher, John Ingram puts it, when it comes to the digitalisation of books, "publishers are still rearranging the deck chairs on the Titanic" "John Ingram on Publishers and Rearranging the Deck Chairs on the Titanic," Interview by Jeremy Greenfield DBW, January 11, 2012, http://www.digitalbookworld.com/2012/john-ingram-on-publishers-and-rearranging-the-deck-chairs-on-the-titanic/. The first e-book was published in 1971 by Michael Hart as a part of the Gutenberg Project—the first producer of free e-books Project Gutenberg, http://www.gutenberg.org/. Apple, Google, and Amazon dominate the market and define the technology that employs restrictive trade practices, with issues of surveillance and privacy, such as keeping a remote access to every downloaded e-book.

Going from paper/print culture to a corporate 'software culture' of publishing, the book—no longer a page but lines of code—is sold as a "license to read." Unlike traditional books, all major e-publishing models allow for a license of use but no ownership. What if we could access the hardware tools of e-reader devices and make a book using a phone's camera for instance? The graphics of e-books still mimic the 'technology' of the book, such as page turning. The online publishing industry is now an oligopoly. Pressured by the drastic economic and technological changes occurring in the publishing industry, how does this affect artistic practice and art institutions?

THE BOOK THAT WRITES ITSELF

Next to this oligopoly coexists a variety and complexity of distribution formats and experiments, redefining data sharing, copying, and authorship. Artists and hacktivists are investigating modes of producing and sharing content, developing open access tools, and addressing corporate monopoly. Aymeric Mansoux, with *Naked on Pluto* Naked on Pluto, http://nimk.nl/eng/naked-on-pluto. *Amazon Noir and Google Will Eat Itself* have been co-authored by UBERMORGEN, Paolo Cirio, Alessandro Ludovico. Face to Facebook is a collaboration between Alessandro Ludovico and Paolo Cirio. Https://paolocirio.net/work/hacking-monopolism-trilogy/.

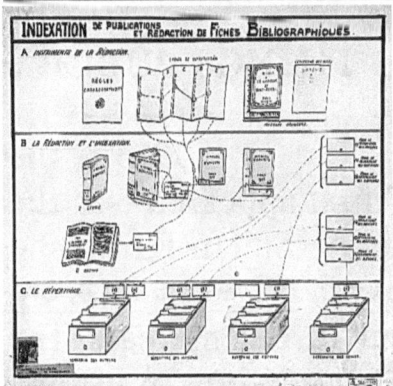

"In all of them, we stole data that is very sensitive for the respective corporations. With Google it was the 'clicks' on their AdSense

115

Program; with Amazon, we started to steal the content of entire books, and with Facebook, we stole a huge amount of public data profiles. In all the three projects, the theft is not used to generate money at all (...) but only to twist the stolen data or knowledge against the respective corporations" "Programming the Book That Writes Itself: Automatically Generating Wikipedia Articles" Christina Sauper, Regina Barzilay, "Automatically generating Wikipedia articles: a structure-aware approach," http://dl.acm.org/citation.cfm?id=1687909 is a research project by Christina Sauper and Regina Barzilay at MIT on text-to-text generation. In his book *Uncreative Writing* Kenneth Goldsmith, *Uncreative Writing: Managing Language in the Digital Age*, Columbia University Press, 2011, Kenneth Goldsmith writes, "Can techniques traditionally thought to be outside the scope of literature, including word processing, databasing, identity ciphering, and intensive programming, inspire the reinvention of writing? The Internet and the digital environment present writers with new challenges and opportunities to reconceive creativity, authorship, and their relationship to language."

MAKING THINGS PUBLIC

1973 is the year the term "artists' books" first appeared—as the title of an exhibition of books. As Stefan Klima Stefan Klima, *Artists Books: A Critical Survey of the Literature*, Granary Books, 1998. points out "but in recent years, the practice has evolved to become a medium in its own right. Three issues dominated the debate: definition, the book considered an object and its challenge to a new kind of reading—the debate's implicit political act, and the desire to challenge an art establishment—the debate's explicit political act". As opposed to the artist book that refers directly to the book as a work of art, 'publishing' transfers the socio-economical, technical, and legal aspects of dissemination of the artist work— the activity of' making it public to a specific audience.

For the artist Aymeric Mansoux, software is the medium. Authorship, textuality, community, access to knowledge and information, and preservation are challenged by corporate practices with their expanded understanding of copyright laws. In this new framework, complex relations and tensions occur between issues of access and privatisation of knowledge, citizenship and new forms of censorship, control, and surveillance. The project Metabook "Metabook—Publishing as Artistic Practice" is an artistic and academic research platform initiated by Delphine Bedel, Leiden University/PhDarts, http:// metabook.institute aims to research and document current publishing practices by artists that are at the confluence of these questions and the possible historiography and archiving of these practices as they emerge. Metabook uses *Anthology* to incorporate artistic practices into the discussion on technology. Publishing is here not an ancillary history—as artists books have been historically documented—but reconsidered as central to emerging artistic practices. *'Anthology,'* according to the philosopher Milad Doueihi Milad Doueihi, *Digital Cultures*, Harvard University Press, 2011., is defined as "constituted by assembling various pieces of material under a unifying cover, and for the use of an individual or a group brought together by a common interest." Anthology is used here as both as a concept, model, and methodology for research.

"Publishing includes the stages of the development, acquisition, copy editing, graphic design, production—printing (and its electronic equivalents), and marketing and distribution" (Wikipedia). The artist/publisher takes on all the roles and reconsiders and transforms their historical definitions.

DRONES, ETC.

Self-publishing responds to a sense of urgency and limited means of production. Online tools and cheaper access to technology allow anyone to become a publisher. Distribution is the main issue that artists and independent publishers are facing. Although the small print runs and the margins of these editions limit their access and audience, many artists have emerged only with their books or online platforms. The New York Art Book Fair had 27,000 visitors last year NYABF, http://nyartbookfair.com/. At times speculative, this interest does not mean that there's an economic 'model' that can be replicated. Publishing is the new home studio—versatile, portable, and accessible, a *community in print*. So where does digitalisation start? The *Invisible Book* by Elisabeth Tonnard was sold out online on the day of release. She wrote: "It is a book produced in a limited edition at the affordable price of € 0. It will work as a digital book too, on any platform" Elisabeth Tonnard, "Invisible Book," http://elisabeth-tonnard.com/works/the-invisible-book/. Publishing will no longer call on the optical nature of an image, where everything is said to make sense of the world, but rather in a reciprocal relation with the audience. Engaging the reader's own sense of touch, emotion, and experience to make sense of an image is what Benjamin used to call the "haptic." Now comes remote publishing, the photographer without a camera and the book without pages. Publishing is just one side of the coin in this revolution in times of satellite surveillance, drones, Google Street View, data ownership and archives preservation, Instagram, and citizen journalism.

THE ANTHROPOLOGY OF COLLECTING

The philosopher and historian Krzysztof Pomian wrote in his *anthropology of collecting* Krzysztof Pomian, *Collectionneurs, amateurs et curieux*, Paris, Venise XVI—XVIIIe siècle', Editions Gallimard, Paris, 1987, pp. 179—180 that in the first auction catalogues in the 17th century, original paintings and their copies were reproduced together. Artists' artwork attributions were often too uncertain but mostly not central to the artwork's commercial value; what mattered was the 'beauty' of the work. Connoisseurs were the ones asserting the value and possible attribution of a work to an artist, based on their own judgment and their knowledge of the 'Principes de la Peinture'. The collection is co-extensive to culture and the privileged vehicle of its transformation. For Pomian, *semiophores* are artefacts removed from economical circulation and practical use but, as referenced objects and carriers of meaning—the 'Invisible'—have a value making them worthy of preservation and display. The collection and exhibition of semiophores mediate between the invisible and visible world (the present). He writes that "in order for the various subsets of society to be able to communicate between each other, they must, among other things, all have access to potential semiophores of the same kind." Kenneth Goldsmith last project, "Printing Out the Internet," is "the first-ever crowd-sourced attempt to literally print out the entire Internet. Over 20,000 people from around the world contributed tens of thousands of pieces of printed Internet." The project steered global online debate and over 1,000 pages of press and commentary Kenneth Goldsmith, "Printing Out the Internet," http://printingtheinternet.tumblr.com/. Collecting, indexing, and sharing all world information was the project of the Mondaneum, a documentation centre initiated in 1910 in Brussels by lawyers Paul Otlet and Henri La Fontaine Mondaneum http://www.google.com/culturalinstitute/exhibit/the-origins-of-the-internet-in-europe/QQ-RRhOA?hl=en. They invented the Universal Decimal Classification System, a system of cards mostly based on books. By 1935, they had 16 million cards, an anticipation of the idea of the Internet. Now the archive is stored away. Are books becoming semiophores or commodities? Google Search Books is a web service that provides access to the text of books and magazines that Google has scanned and converted to text using optical character recognition Google Search Books, http://en.wikipedia.org/wiki/Google_Books. For Google, the future of their corporate endeavour to digitalise libraries all over the world is not to create universal access to culture but aims at the potential for books to be read by *machines*.

ECHO 2—TOWARD AN AESTHETIC OF DELAY

Lars Bang Larsen <u>after a text by
Søren Andreasen and Lars Bang Larsen</u>

Imagine that you are.

Imagine that you are surrounded by nothing but echoing. Besides how you might feel—pleased, indifferent, disorientated—you are left in a reality of reverberations.

When there is echoing, there is time and space. It is an effect of a delay in time and space, a signal that drifts while it repeats and mutates.

To understand the echo's offense, we must ask what kind of sign echoing is—if it indeed is one? By definition, a sign is something that is repeatable: A sign which does not repeat itself, which is not already divided by repetition, is not a sign.

In order to refer to the same thing each time, the signifying referral therefore must be ideal—as ideality is the assured power of repetition. But by being an impure repetition that fades and grows old as it undermines substantial form, echoing is a mockery of the sign's ideality. It repeats a source by turning it into something else: sound-matter, spatialized time, a saturated sign in excess of itself. At the same time, weirdly, echoing is not non-repetition because it sticks to its source. The echo is new and not new, it is life and non-life, synthetic and not-created, I and not-I. As it mutates, it clings and reveals your position in time and space by answering back with a voice that it borrowed from you. The echo is sign and material: a sign because it communicates, a material because it is perceptible and non-ideal. Echoing is the opposite of growth and accumulation: it is reminiscent of the interest of a debt that keeps nibbling at a principal, or one can compare it to an originary speech-act or sound-act that yields diminishing returns.

But even understood as sign-material, the echo is tricky. What happens when somebody produces echoing? And why would anyone want to pursue such an objective in the first place?

In the twentieth century, it was held that art could become the heart of humanity by negating spectacle and empty appearance, and by healing fragmentation and fissure. In that perspective, echoing is the worst thing that could happen. It unsettles the body and humbles free will. It is a movement without essence that defies mastery—a mess, the cancellation of Utopia. The American art historian Clement Greenberg, italicizing his disgust, described how in the abstract painter Barnett Newman's paintings "… the picture edge is repeated inside and makes the picture, instead of merely being *echoed*."

But what if mastery couldn't be achieved in time and space due to the echo's treason? Then there was another argument that would save you from being sent howling out into the void. It went: never mind, let us simply abjure the world instead.

Let the world ring out into the nothingness it came from. Utopianism and nihilism—two sides of the same coin—are symptoms of the inability to make peace with a space-time that, in one way or another, refuses transcendence.

The echo disturbs claims to transparency. As Henri Lefebvre said of the Situationist movement's practice of frequent expulsions amongst its members, "It was really about keeping oneself in a pure state, like a crystal." To keep oneself in an echo-free state necessitates the suppression of the reverberations that one's engagement has in everything that isn't governed by law. Consequently, to embrace echoing is to increase the probability of your corruption, your impregnability in the present. The echo is spongy, not crystalline.

One of the twentieth-century art forms that let the echo in was Op Art. Here, the painted patterns of swelling or warping produce impressions of movement, hidden images, flashing, and vibration, generating a suggestive experience of space which is based on a mix of geometry, perception psychology, and constructivist design. In an Op Art piece, geometry constitutes an imagery of optical tricks and stylish surfaces that neglect the symbolic status of geometry as a Primary Structure, warping this transcendent idealism into an affective spatiality which is close to hallucination.

Serial Form is another artistic attitude that injected echoing into the volume of space. These modular-based sculptures are defined by a succession of moves, all of equal value and controlled by the anticipation of future movements of the parts. It is a serial principle of 'internal repetition'—a successive delay between sequence and progression—that almost literally short-circuits the unity and coherence of space, producing an impression of an ever-growing synthesis of volume that is explicitly opposed to 'Platonic virtues' and 'Minimalism's purist-type homage to industrial production.'

Also, the psychedelic imagery and agency of the 1960s belong to this line of art, not only because it employed similar compositional and stylistic features, but also through a radical emphasis on the materiality of experience. Here, the art piece's suggestive space stimulated impressions of an expanded space which was translated into media freak-outs, demonstrations, and acid tests. You could even call this decade's drug fascination a kind of reverberation in the Primary Structures of cultural and social space: a lot of minds and bodies were chemically swelling and warping in protest. Feedback—the acid rock feedback—is the apotheosis of the echo: it is the electrified monster echo with a proclivity for displacing the musician who started the process that is the feedback whine, the space in which it is played, and for cannibalizing its own children—always growing, ever changing.

What these practices have in common is their desire to open up to suggestive spatialities which are situated simultaneously in reality's physical properties and in the ideality of conceptual powers. They constitute spaces that can only be measured by the time-scale of experience, as they are neither directly present to the senses nor fully accessible to conceptual powers. The impure nature of the echo might thus be thought of in terms of ambivalence, indirection, and synthesis; the echo is an indication of a space which you can only get access to through the delayed experience of echoing.

In the world of sound production, the artificial echo has a primal scene in the work of the American producer Phil Spector. In the early 1960s, he created a simple 'machine' to add echoing effects to his recordings; to re-record already recorded sounds; a microphone and a loudspeaker were placed at each end of a narrow corridor formed by two metal plates. An infinite variety of reverberation effects could be generated by adjusting this arrangement and by endless re-recording.

Echo ambiance was a popular feature of pop music long before Spector, but was until then produced by using the acoustics of accessible spaces for live sessions, such as empty cinemas, theaters, or churches. Since Spector, the producer has controlled the definition of specific sound qualities in the studio.

The question is what happens to the echo when it is deliberately produced. Keeping in mind the recording techniques of Phil Spector, is it still true that, as we write in the above, 'When there is an echo, there is time and space'? What kind of time and space does the echo of two metal plates in a studio indicate—that of the echo machine? In a way, yes, since the method of production is a reference in itself, in Spector's case, The Wall of Sound, his trademark style. But this technique also functions as a way to work independently of accessible space and to echo any imaginable structure. You could call this hypothetical time and space, brought about by the realities of the echo machine(s) and the psychological and social being of the producer(s). But the hypothetical time and space are still separate from the latter by not being determined by psychology or social space.

Of course, Spector didn't make his echo machine hypothetically. It was cutting-edge sound equipment in the service of the pop industry. But it remains that 'echo production' involves the producer in a very direct way: echoing simply would not exist unless someone had decided to produce it. In some cases, the decision to make an echo is a way to recognize oneself: a way to think and act when one cannot or will not recognize oneself in relation to accessible time and space, or when one can only recognize oneself in relation to hypothetical time and space. One can even call it a continuous un-working of the possible.

In this way, the production and consumption of echoing are at the same time a negation and an anticipation of accessible time and space. We can define hypothetical time and space as a dimension inside accessible time and space where structures of distortion, speculation, and pleasure are brought about by somebody's discomfort, ability, or playfulness. This type of agency is never neutral, because its ideas and actions aim at establishing themselves in tomorrow's world through their resonance in people and symbolic exchange, and in markets and institutions.

Graham Harman notes that "the real is something that cannot be known, only loved." Harman calls the sense-making human subject a 'hunter of objects.' But we are non-lethal hunters "since objects can never be caught": objects are ghostly and "withdrawing from all human and inhuman access, accessible only by allusion and seducing us by means of allure." Graham Harman, "The Third Table." In Bakargiev (ed.), *The Book of Books*. Kassel, 2012, Documenta, pp. 540–542. Whatever we *capture*—by verification, by commodification, or by instrumentalization—is not the real. The real can only be speculated forth, if we understand speculation as a loving gesture. However, Harman's orientation towards objects doesn't gel with processes and delays, with uncontrollable recurrences in anachronistic spaces, which is what we are concerned with here.

Echoing undoes the pseudo-event, which is the attempt to command the passing of historical time through the still exploitable signs of authenticity and originality. Countless apparatuses—institutions, commercial mechanisms, mass media, professional media—are poised to restrain, calculate and master time, only to speed it up again jerkily by delivering irresistibly authoritative countdowns and build-ups to the Next Big Thing. These time machines are the reducers, the distractors, the non-listeners. When they have been at it, there is always a need to start again.

We will revisit anything that is considered so last year if it is relevant, if we feel like it, for the hell of it. Not because we will become sharper or our knowledge will be more complete at a future point in time, but because we can pool and crowd our utterances. You cannot regain and improve what already circulates. Instead, one can consider what has already been said from where the said now circulates.

Even if it circulates and is mediated, it will be reconsidered and worked through once more. This is a way to make an argument denser, to make it hold out against the time machines. It is how echoing becomes a recourse to the absolute—even if this absolute may be nothing more than a stumbling block, a redundancy. Unlike the despondent calls of that pathetic Greek nymph, this movement is anything but melancholic as long as it contains a measure of destruction (or self-mockery and self-critique, in so far as it is self-destruction).

To re-open closed cases, to drift away, to work with versioning is to set originals free from authorship and permanence—one of those most difficult tasks, in fact, to release art and the aesthetic experience from the hold that the eternal continues to exert over them. It is not to see things *sub specie aeternitatis*, but to see them *sub specie quodlibet*; not under the aspect of eternity, but under the aspect of whatever.

We are not done. Nothing is signed—by you, me, anybody. Once we realize that the things we have created don't belong to ourselves, we will be in a position to produce a movement of our own. We have no idea what is yet to be done. What will happen, will happen in time.

Stay tuned.

This is the third version of the text originally written by Søren Andreasen and Lars Bang Larsen as a catalog essay for *The Echo Show* (Tramway, Glasgow 2003) and subsequently re-edited by both for the book *The Critical Mass of Mediation* (2012/2014).

BREAKFAST WITH BIFO
Franco Bifo Berardi and Andrea Marioni

[…]

ANDREA MARIONI: Hello this is [LapTopRadio's] *Back in '12* special morning broadcasting. We are always in Kassel, Germany, at Documenta 13. And this special *Back in '12* Radio show is with a guest who has already presented some of his work in Documenta: Franco Bifo Berardi. It's breakfast time, we just woke up, so we don't want to go very fast. We just want to take our time and to share it with you as much as possible. I will just ask our guest how he is doing, and then we'll just listen to one or two other songs so we can finish our breakfast.

Hello Bifo, thank you for accepting to be here. I chose this song Lavorare con lentezza by Enzo Del Re for many reasons. First because [… in the LapTopRadio context] I have discovered your work, through the movie *Lavorare con lentezza*. That was like six months ago so I am happy to be with you now. And also I chose this song because it's the morning and I want to work slowly and take my time. So yes, how are you?

FRANCO BIFO BERARDI: I'm fine. Thank you. We have just one microphone, so we have to work slowly as in the song *Lavorare con lentezza*. It's an Old Song of a Neapolitan Singer called Enzo del Re, a singer who was well known in Italy in the 70s. Hmm, well known I'm not sure. In some "milieu" he was well

known in that period, and I belonged to the same mi
lieu, the milieu of people who wanted to work slowly
and people who don't like hyper speed and exploita
tion. Soooooo have a good morning.

[...]

AM: Let's start with a first question for
Bifo. I would like to ask you if you can shortly bring
us back to the time of *Radio Alice*, and say some words
about that time? How it began? And now after 40 years
what is your memory of this experience?

BB: Well, we are talking
about the 70s, and to be more precise about 74-75. And
the time, the period, the age of *Radio Alice* is the age
of social movements, social conflicts in Italy, and not
only in Italy. But it is also the period of the deep re
cession, the deep crisis which in a sense changed the
perception of work, of social relations... after 73, the
oil shocks, the sudden increase of oil prices, jeopard
ized the economy in the world, and the consequences
of that was a wave of unemployment among young
people and the beginning of what we now call precar
ious work. The classical industrial relation in a sense
was broken after 73.   This is the gener
al frameworks of what happened in Italy. In Italy, af
ter 73 and until 77, a large, a strong wave of social move
ments and of violent conflicts is shaking the schools
the factories, the cities. *Radio Alice* is one of the many
events of that period.

Radio Alice is of special interest in the point
of view of the history of communication. Of course it

is the first free radio in Italy, I would say in Europe, with the exception of the United Kingdom. Until 75 the communication, the TV broadcast, the radio broadcast was a State business. Only the State, only the official organizations of the national states were allowed to broadcast on the airwaves. In 75 a window of possibility was opened for legal questions, all of a sudden it was possible to broadcast and to create a radio.

A group of people, students, young workers, young artists started a radio station in Bologna, which is the first free radio station in Italy. The beginning of the broadcasting is in February 76. And you can guess that if you now want to listen to a radio, you can choose between thousands of possibilities, so broadcasting on the radio or TV is no more such an extraordinary event. But on February 9, 1976 the fact that in the ether, in the airwaves a group of strange people who were not the official representative of the Italian State were saying strange things in a microphone and in the radio receivers of people was kind of a scandal. So in a few days *Radio Alice* reached an audiences of 40,000 people in the city of Bologna, which is a huge number by normal standards, and *Radio Alice* became the voice of the movement, of the students, of the unemployed, of the autonomy, of those people who were revolting against the austerity, against the situation of unemployment, precarity, social misery. And the activity of Radio Alice grew during the year 76. In 77 the movement became a true insurrection in Rome, in Bologna and in many Italian cities. The fight between students and the state, the police and the political organizations of the establishment became so strong, so violent that we can speak about a true insurrection of Italian young people. And *Radio Alice* was deeply involved in this process, until the day March 12, 1977 when the police entered the radio station, arrested all the people that were inside the radio station and closed the radio. Well, this is the short story of *Radio Alice*. Actually the story is not finished, because the radio opened the day after and the police closed it again…. It's kind of the story of the beginning of free information in Italy. And, forty years after, it can be perceived as the legendary history of the origin of something that nowadays is widespread, not only on the radio, but also on the internet.

[…]

AM: Yes of course. We don't have today as much audience as *Radio Alice* had. But I'll maybe engage with the question of the group of *Radio Alice* as dilettantes, since media was a monopoly of the state. Perhaps today some artists are using this position of dilettante to try to find out another way to deal with a subject or something like this. So my question will be about these, I won't say amateurs, but maybe people who don't really know how to do radio. Since you were in this practice yourself, with this kind of new media, could you say some words about how you have learned during this time, when you were a dilettante and you "occupied" a media.

BB: You know the 70s were not only a decade of social conflict and of change in the economy and society. The 70s were also the decade of change in the learning process in the formation of a new generation of people who started creating and learning at the same time what now we call the new technologies. A large number of technicians, engineers started to mix with the activists, the militants, the poets, the artists, the intellectuals. And there were also phenomena like the citizen band, the bricolage of electronics, the starting of the computer sciences in the 70s. Some of my friends, some of the people who create Radio Alice, were studying electronic engineering and started creating the first computer project. You know Steve Jobs and Steve Wozniak in California have created the Apple trade mark in the year 77.

77 is a marking year not only in the cultural political point of view, but also in the technological, scientific point of view. In a sense the 70s have been the starting point of the revolution that we now are living as daily life, as something normal.

So the learning process has been a collective process of discovering possibilities which were emerging with the diffusion of the electronics. Electronic is the keyword of the 70s, not so much Digital. Digital and Network are words that came on the scene in the 80s or 90s, but the Electronic revolution is the soul, the technological soul of that process which is also the process of creation of the free radio, in a technological point of view.

In the same time these people, that in that age we called the *Technikwissenschaftsintelligenz* a german expression, because in Germany there was a theoretician called Hans Jürgen Krahl, Frankfurt based student, leader of this movement. Hans Jurgen Krahl was speaking of this new class which was the

Technikwissenschaftsintelligenz, the intelligentsia, the intellectuality of people who were not only intellectuals but also technicians. He saw in this new class the possibility of a deep change in social relationship and social conflict. If you see what happened after 1970, technology has played a crucial role in that change. Not only in economy, but also in the change of social consciousness and in the change of our political possibilities.

ON AND AROUND TIME
Alfredo Cramerotti

I once had a colleague, Maria, who used to read two-year-old newspapers every evening at home. Everyone at the office, including myself, would often joke about this rather peculiar pastime of hers.

Today, I see things differently. It seems to me that the whole matter of reading newspapers from the past is a wise move: an act of foreseeing the future rather than a retrospective one. Reading an old daily broadsheet can give you a chill, whether out of fear or excitement, about how history—as the historicization of facts or rather opinions through mainstream media outputs—is an ongoing construct.

I partake in this process only if I decide to seize some distance and use this 'gap' to continually undermine and reconstruct its proceedings.

Delaying the act of decoding information can lead to the re-appropriation of aspects in my daily life. Furthermore, embracing this time-space distance can be considered as an artistic reading of reality—the here and now seen tangentially. Indeed this puts what has been said, done or thought into a broader perspective, which in turn allows space for 'lateral thinking.' This extra layer of thought ultimately informs and gives insight into what to do next, rather than what was done before. In treating the reality of the world as a series of constructed events, I reinvent my daily reality. I read any landscape, fact or situation as though it were an artwork.

To read life in delay is not a matter of fabricating (the present) or documenting (the past) but simply about embracing one among the many possibilities of awareness; being aware is the essence of participation. I wrote in another text that we start to get closer to the core of our reality not when we represent it (or absorb its representation) but when we consider it as a possibility among many others and not as a given, irreversible fact. I subscribe to this statement.

Only when I engage with the possibility of something can I try to change what is important (for me). It is a matter of adding knowledge, connecting what I already know with what I do not know, placing the new (old) in sequence with other knowledge.

Maria, through her evenings spent in the re-actualizing of the past, has taught me in a great yet subtle way that life is not so much about who I am now, but who I will become—it is projected towards the future rather than an agency of the past. It is a question of how I choose to think of myself. I do not possess time, neither can I dispose of it, I can only inhabit it wholly. At this moment, while you read these words, I am your time.

Likewise, reality is not a fact to be understood but rather an effect to be produced, in which you and I are embedded. So, when I go home tonight, I will take a

1997 edition of La Repubblica, just to name a newspaper that I used to read, I will spread it out on the floor; perhaps skip the weather report (but you never know), and then read the articles that will tell me how my life is going to change. I will position things in perspective and recollect choices, thoughts, and opinions.

And I will perhaps have the feeling that the past is still in progress, and that I have never really been able to remove myself from within it. Just like now.

This essay was first elaborated for *Transmission Journal*. Published on the occasion of *SI Sindrome Italiana MAGASIN-Centre National d'Art* Contemporain, Grenoble 10-10-2010 / 02-01-2011.

THE CULT OF THE RAMMELLZEE
Joël Vacheron

Based on a discussion between Tex Royale, Alexis Milne (>>THE CULT OPERATORS>>) and Joël Vacheron

EQUATION

I am a student of the Rammellzee. HIS work is my homework. HE leaves *tracks* called *lectures,* and it does not matter that HE is dead. Like HE says in interviews, the *RAMM:$\sum LL$:$Z\sum\sum$* is an equation, HE is not a person. HE never speaks to anyone as the Rammellzee but as other spirits and entities that HE wishes to channel. Maybe this is part of the *rhizomatic nature* of the equation. HE did a real good job at keeping HIS 'actual human identity' quite secret.

WILD STYLE

HE has always been an innovative force and the outfits that HE produces remind us of graffiti art pieces. In particular, the *Wild Style,* which developed in New York over a thirty-year period. *Wild Style* was the name applied to the abstract wild graffiti art on trains, the 'pinnacle' of that graffiti art culture at that time. What came out of Hip-hop visually, HE *translates* it physically and spiritually. HIS philosophy *springboards* out of that, and his outfits become a 3D embodiment of the *evolution* of Wild Style. The Wild Style evolves off of HIS exoskeleton. The letters are being freed from the alphabet's printed form. HE relates it back to the monks. That's HIS philosophy: *Gothic Futurism.*

HE penetrates the pinnacle and arms it from the inside out, rewiring it until it functions as a medieval amphibious tank. HE states that Gothic Futurism is Wild Style corrected. Wild Style letters are a larval form. The Rammellzee is the trans-galactic shamanic executive gangster collective, overseeing and orchestrating this process.

BLASTING OFF

HE talks about aerodynamics, aeronautics, and all these... technical mechanics.

HE talks about *weaponizing* the letter, turning it into craft that can fly;

the letters will have wings, the letters will *fly off* the pages. These letters are of aerodynamic design. HE tells us to look at the church steeples, how they're designed to take off. Blasting off, being hi-power mechanised—these are feats of engineering and precision. When we perform *break~spraying*, it allows the energy of a letterform to break loose and decide itself by manipulating the chassis of a human body; we put the letter in the driving seat.

CHAOS

The Rammellzee talks about the *equation*. A letter is a symbol that *represents energy*. The energy manifests as sound when we communicate with spoken language.

What people call *graffiti* is part of a struggle to allow that energy to break free from the recognized forms that it's been trapped in. What we do within the Cult, the performance that we do, the costumes that we make, the totemic structures... whatever it is within the performance; none of it is polished, none of it is refined, none of it is clean or tidy. It's very chaotic.

HUE-MANS

The Rammellzee was not content with the idea of Afro-futurism; HE didn't even believe in it, stating that it doesn't exist. HE plays with language, and when talking about humans, HE identifies the sly components of the word, singling out the sounds of what we hear, visualizing this as *hue-mans*. HE traces the origins of graffiti back beyond the seventeenth century monks, entwining it with the history of the illuminated manuscripts and that evolution. HIS work is a continuation of that tradition and its evolution. When was the last time that a white western art movement was defined by a haircut? We'll see you in six years once we've got *Quiffmysticism* in full-scale automated operation.

OBSCURE

Gothic Futurism appears to be impenetrable. This is part of HIS strategy. There are not enough scholars and time out there to break the code and it's going to take a long time for people

to consider that material seriously so that it fully digests mentally on the *collective scale*. Here's the longevity and what makes it timeless. When people do engage, they're going to get it wrong—this is why the Cult works so well. We *over-identify* with

Ritual Documentation 2004

these things, and we get it *wrogn*. What we do is a *mis-interpretation*. The Cult is not of this time, and through our performances, we are re-enacting something that happens in a potential future, a different timeline. We're interpreting this material through frosted glass. You see a vague shape but have to make up the rest.

DISTANCE

We never met HIM in person, and so in that way we are at a distance. We didn't grow up in the Bronx or the South of Queens, in this dystopian background of New York at that time. We do have this so-called *strategy of over-identification*, and the direction we take is the idea of *ingesting* that culture from a distance, which is both spatially and chronologically energized, as well as otherwise. There is this retranslation of it from across the ocean, and distance does enable you to open up some space to create something new as well.

ALIEN

The Rammellzee is a renaissance figure within Hip-hop. HE was a graffiti writer and a rapper, mastering the written and spoken word. In a kind of symbiotic feedback loop relationship, HE would freestyle conscious streams of rap responding to break-dance moves that were happening in front of HIM, communicating this wild aggressive dance-form to the crowd, even conjuring it. HE was an embodiment of this weird alien Hip-hop form, which seemingly came out of nowhere, an active and reactive node of its projection—evidence of our cosmic origin. Where did that cultural explosion come from exactly? Sure it has lineages back to all these other older forms of freeform Jazz and Soul dance, but breaking, popping, locking; it all accelerated forward into a distinct future body zone. We are the future. The future is now. The future ain't what it used to be... in Baudrillard's essay *Kool Killer*, you get this idea that the subway train graffiti movement was a violent onslaught by a whole youth group, a disenfranchised neglected section of society in New York.

The graffiti writers were a resilient anti-force that operated *against* the symbolic order of signs. Its true meaning lost to the untrained eye, the alien script engulfed an entire rapid transit system like a virus and transmitted an image of New York as a city at war with itself. It was a brief but violent 'insurrection of signs.' In other documentaries and questionable films of that period (late 1970s to mid 80s), New York is depicted as a lawless hellhole, and graffiti-ridden trains are used as a prominent symbol amongst the rubble mounds of the Bronx. Films such as *Death Wish, Wolfen, Forte Apache, The Bronx...* What we're looking at is illuminated alien expression from an openly oppressed and alienated nation.

"I am Chaser the Eraser, restaurateur, maître 'd to the Plasmatics." The Rammellzee allows beings to talk through HIM, in HIS work, in HIS performances. HE idolizes them, makes costumes, figurines for each one of them. It's HIS pantheon. HE is THEM and maybe is best referred to as THEY. Let's talk a little about voodoo rituals. When a *Loa* is successfully summoned, it *mounts* or *rides* a human being who is present at the ritual. The mounted take on the personas of the different Loa. Once someone is mounted, and the Loa is identified, they are given their familiars, perhaps a certain kind of hat or cane… The Loa each possess a *style*, purpose, and personality of their own. The mounted take on traits *way* contrary to their day-to-day self, performing acts that would normally stop them dead in their tracks. Modern psychologists got no real explanation for how these kinds of possessions work, how this mounting takes effect.

It doesn't matter if a Loa decides to take residence up in a rock or if they choose to rest inside a toy plastic gun—it's not correct to identify the Loa as being *of* said object, be it a tree, a sneaker, or a car bumper. It's not like *"hark hark, 'tis Bark, the Loa of the Log"*— no, the Loa are *transient* beings from beyond—*Archetypical Archons*, to whom we are eternally receptive as vessels, for they dwell deep within our collective *exo-consciousness*. Take the Ghede family from Haitian voodoo mythology. They embody death and fertility, creation and destruction. You meet *Papa Ghede* at the *crossroads*. He cares for the children, and will never take a life before its time is due. He wears dark smoked glasses with one lens missing, so one eye can see the entire universe and this other eye can make sure that no one is stealing his food.

TRANS-RAPPER

Trans- has a lot of different meanings; it's a transition, a kind of permeation from one state to another or from one place to another. And the Rammell-zee was definitely *a trans-rapper*. HE wasn't just trans-gender. HE would perform sometimes as the Duchess, a female figure, but HE was trans-human to an extent. Not like the Futurist notion of a singularity merging with the machine mind either. That's a false prophecy of the oppressors. HE let these ancient voices speak through HIM. It's like Rupaul says, *"We're all born naked, and the rest is drag."* Drag racing. Letter racing. HE was taking language, taking the letter, the vocal sound and turning these 'natural human things' into a technology, turning it into a tool, into a weapon against the oppressive forces. That's *spectral somatechnics of the soul.*

Graffiti art developed on subway trains, and it transmitted a suppressed language from a whole group of disenfranchised youth and fused untrained letters with moving steel, energized with electric voltage, utilizing a dynamic platform—a mass rapid transit system, which is how the Rammellzee comes into fruition for these performances. It's like quantum mechanics combined with original subway train writing, combined with shock flashbacks of future vision. In 2013, the Cult performed a ritual under the West Way, the huge brutalist road, which runs through Ladbroke Grove, where graffiti first landed from New York in 1981. The first New York graffiti piece was painted on the huge concrete legs of the Westway by FUTURA2000 whilst on tour with The Clash (elements of Hip-hop and Punk overlap momentarily).

FUTURA is known for his abstract graffiti; he re-animated the concrete, which obviously seemed alien and inhuman, but graffiti had the power to reenergize it, to *remanipulate* it. You get that *trans-* momentum again, a *trans-morphing*. All this feeds into the methodologies we create within the Cult—especially with the *Feral ExpresSways* sub-cult. The West Way ritual paid homage to that first piece and its subsequent viral effects. The West Way covers an important area for London graffiti culture—the elevated road provided huge concrete pillars for the first graffiti pieces to exist. The huge Brutalist concrete road along with hi-rise estates (such as Trellick Tower) was also the backdrop to the elevated section of the inner metropolitan tube train line, where London graffiti artists would *translate* their own version of the New York transit script onto London Underground *moving steel*. The viral ripple continues. Of course, little or nothing remains of the UK's initial graffiti onslaught except in documentation; it has been chemically wiped clean, or *buffed* as graffiti writers say. Anti-bodied. Body slammed. Sometimes a stain of that period will remain however. The Bitumen that's used as the binding agent of concrete is also used to make spray paint more permanent. Bitumen has a staining effect and would stain tube trains and walls with resilient ghost tags and pieces unwilling to disappear. *'Asphalt Bitumen'* is another mantra the Cult chant. We celebrate this resilient bio-agent of destruction and creation, the link between the concrete expressways and urban viral onslaught.

SECOND WORLD WAR RUBBLES

When you watch the documentaries about Hip-hop and this era (*Style Wars, Wild Style, Stations of the Elevated*), the subculture is framed against the dystopian backdrop of the South Bronx, which was largely reduced to piles of rubble and burnt bricks, a scene from a Second World War documentary, aerial shots of a bombed-out Dresden at the end of civilization. Often, in the footage, you have a rusty subway train running through a burnt-out wasteland, covered top to bottom with anarchic alien script scrawled and crafted across the chassis, hurtling through the aftermath of gentrification. In the Cult, we focus on that *rubble trauma.*

MOZIZIZM

The Cult concentrates on Robert Moses, the major *Archonitect* of the Cross Bronx Expressway, a road of major importance within Hip-hop. Many key events took place in a *seven-mile radius* of this expressway... The first important Block parties where iconic DJs like Kool Herc, Grandmaster Flash, and Afrika Bambaataa were cutting up, scratching, and mixing records for the first time. You also had the subway station on 149th Street, known as *The Bench*—this would be the main meeting area and hang out joint to watch freshly painted masterpiece subway graffiti roll by on wheels of steel across the number 2 and 5 lines.

In the Cult, Moses becomes MOZIZIZM, taking on God-like proportions alongside the Rammellzee and becoming a key element of the equation, almost to the point where he is responsible for the creation of Hip-hop. He created these void spaces within the city following the motto: *'when operating in an over built metropolis, you've got to hack your way through with a meat axe.'* Eighty percent of the South

Bronx moved out during the building of The Cross Bronx Expressway and the ensuing policies of neglect. Moses cut up entire neighborhoods. Cut people off from vital resources like fire stations, hospitals, and schools. Split up families and communities, injecting these ghetto spaces. There was a policy of neglect and a policy of division. Moses redirected funds away from Rapid Mass Transit into expressway building, always favoring auto-individualism above mass transversal. That's what we mean by *the Shiny Ones*. Public transport was left to deteriorate, which lay bare subway train yards and lay ups ready to receive the fifth dimensional step parallel staircase delivered by the ghetto monks, the wild style script manipulators such as CLIFF159, FUZZ, IZ, PHASE2, CAINE, BLADE, COMET, KASE2, THE DEATH SQUAD, SKEME, NOC, A-ONE, FUTURA2000, DONDI, VULCAN and all those who now *ZIP!* along the third rail—the electromagnetic majestix. Zoom In Peace. Moses was the *MOLOCH*, the '*concrete sphinx of cement and aluminum,*' and these figures permeate into our rituals. We do *express-prays* devoted to *MOZIZIZM*.

PLASMATIC

Because of its heavily encrypted codes, its algebraic formulas and equations, its plays with language, Gothic Futurism is difficult to penetrate. What you can do is look at the things HE was looking at—yo, or who was looking at *HIM*. The legendary Bill Burroughs knew HIM as his FATHER—and likewise the Rammellzee knew Bill as HIS SON. Bill was very aware of the *operator entities* who flip from body to body. He wasn't alone either—for instance, take the works of Philip K. Dick. Dick got a trilogy of books; one of the books is *VALIS* (Vast Active Living Intelligence System).

The story, which is fictional to an extent, documents a period of Dick's life and talks about a being called the *plasmate*. Living information. Information actualized as an entity. That is what the Ancient Greeks called the *logos*. VALIS, or the plasmate, is also referred to as *Zebra* because of its ability to camouflage from human perception, appearing as aspects of your day-in-day-out reality—appearing as other humans, appearing as trashcans, as pipes, as pot... whatever. There are different kinds of camouflage, higher and lower, what the plasmate is capable of is a *hi-level mimesis*. Dick explores the idea that this *plasmate* can form a symbiosis with a human, forming a *homoplasmate*. He talks about Jesus and other religious figures as humans who became *homoplasmate*. The Rammellzee talks about the *Plasmatics* in a very nonchalant matter-of-fact manner, like it's a given that they are a real day-to-day aspect of existence and experience. It's clear to see here ties between the plasmate and the Loa, the Loa and the logos. Living Information that has learned how to *operate the human*. What happens when a Loa bounds itself to its human mount instead of letting go at the end of the ceremony? When the glove melds in with the skin? Have you seen the colony of human tissue, the hybrid with spider silk? It can take a hit from a bullet, no puncture. It's happening. Humans are gonna reawaken to the Hylozoic elephant in the room. For then, we speculate that the Rammellzee is a live example of a plasmatic entity operating humanity in our un-distant history.

CROCODILIAN FORMS

"WE'RE LIKE ANCIENT FOSSILS, HENRY—WE DON'T LEAVE TIME, TIME LEAVES US!" Recently we've moved into including crocodilian forms, combined with the idea of a feral expressway. It's the concrete becoming animated; we come out on all fours with road shapes on our bodies, snarling and drooling in the heat of the beast. People commented that we resemble dog-like crocodile creatures when we do this.

If you look at our ancient biology, there are species *in-between* crocodile and dog, the missing links between reptile and mammal. Mammalian lizards. They emerged out of a fertile period, approximated in relation to the Triassic, when dinosaurs were 'dying out.' Certain creatures, like crocodiles and dogs, survived the wrath of the Titans. All our ancient cousins blossomed and flourished in full bloom, but they would eventually dissolve with the dinosaurs and become the tar pits, where asphalt and oil would form. That's the matmos. It is true that ultimately we are all made out of goo. Asphalt is being used as the binding concrete. The concrete is literally made out of their remains. JAPLACK Stains remain. They are a link to the formation of *"the petroleum vitamins—Asphalt Bitumens— the eternal stain ain't slain again."*

EXOSKELETON

The exoskeletons, that's part of our *rad manifest*. Now, when one is obsessed with *style*, this can be very difficult *but!* it is important, when talking about aesthetics, to try not to tie the meaning of that down to just how something looks. It's the driving force within the rituals as well. The Plasmatics have *created* these characters. The costumes aren't simply exoskeleton—they are the visible residual of our *exo-consciousness*.

HOOVERZ BOYZ

Yeah there are sub-cults within the Cult, like the *Feral ExpresSway Pack* (those are the crocodile concrete Cult kids), and the *Hooverz Boyz*, aka the *Dysonix*—that's if you wanna camo the ammo flaps and pack a mask on that. They're a representation of our Intelligence Agencies: *Hooverz Boyz, see!* And they do! These Hooverz Boyz represent Jay Edgar Hoover's *COINTELPRO*, counter intelligence, the *dirty tricks* program. One of the best ways that the Hooverz Boyz can be performed is with broken or remanipulated hoovers, so that rather than just like sucking stuff up and putting it in a bag, they suck stuff up and shoot it back out. So you have these things like the intelligence agencies *'cleaning things up, cleaning up the mess. Nothing to see here.'* But they're just creating more mess, and they are very dangerous. Chuck D has a lyric in one of his tracks: *'the CIA, they see I ain't kidding.'* The Intelligence Agencies are all over.

COMMUNAL ECSTASY

All the successful rituals have boosted the crowd into this communal ecstasy. When we are in ritual trance; sometimes people go crazy. In Rotterdam, we were walking down the streets, and those who joined the Cult after the show, they wouldn't stop shouting the chants. They're doing mantras; they're shouting out in the street, in the club, the shops, at home, wherever! They've started dancing and praying, doing the movements and the motions and everything. It's always this kind of temporary, ephemeral moment, but these moments can mark consciousness. You can empower moments.

ECSTATIC CHAOS

It's a *communal frenzy*, that's how we've called it, but there is choreography within it. Certain movements we know, we practice. Others just happen. It's an ecstatic chaos. It's like conducting; within sections of the chaos, there's a brass section in the chaos; that's the *Ferals* or the *Dysonix*, forming something within that chaos, reconfiguration. It's like breakdancing; it's like you wind the body up with this energy of the break beat. In the performances, it's tapping into that. A wild breaking, not totally choreographed and polished; it's a charged moment—motion led by momentum, bodies merging, going mindless so you might get mounted.

TOTEMIC SHAPES

We produce totemic shapes with found or scavenged car bumpers, and a Cultist will pull a headstand and freeze, while the rest of the Cult holds up all this scrap shrapnel so we become like a, a... *siphonophoric human ziggurat.* Which points back to breakdancing, some kind of head freeze, like just about going into a headspin, but you are holding that. You're not going through that same motion. And then this totemic shape will happen with other members of the Cult.

 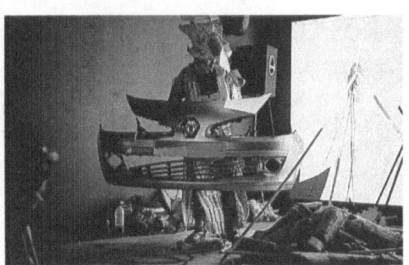

We all have these bulky exoskeleton outfits on, our Plasmatic outfits, which together as a whole can produce this other abstract form within a section in the ritual. That's why it's like the *Siphonophorae*, from the Order of Hydrozoa—sure they might *look* like a jellyfish, but that's not even one animal! They're all together, like in a cult.

SPRAY~BREAKING

There is spray~breaking, which is pointing towards breakdancing but trying to combine it with elements of freeform bombing, using spray paint to mark surfaces. It's ritualistic and expressive, spraying on the floor in black on some lino, which is being used *right now* for breakdancing in the eighties. We'll have cut out mats along strips of it, long mats, then we'll be spraying and attempting to breakdance at the same time—spray~breaking. It's sloppy and spasmodic in its energy. We're not regurgitating a breakdancing move within a theatrical performance. We want to channel all those different energies into these new forms. The break spraying is a physically exhausting means of doing that because you're using your whole body. It becomes this kind of playing in your own filth and reveling in it while breathing in the gasses of the Oracle of Delphi. It's like we said before, the letter takes control. A spray~breaker makes that plasmatic connection—the lino becomes a *Ouija board*, and the marks you make trace micro ley lines of psychic writing. Yeah, you lose a part of yourself and transform that moment or transverse into some other form.

SORROW

One of the things that comes up a lot, that a lot of people that we know who have seen our performances comment on, is that it is often quite sad. There's often these huge waves of sorrow, and some of the time people get scared, get frightened. And fear and sorrow is not something that it is our purpose or intent to express, but we are projecting this image of a future in which the highways and the roads and the concrete, the asphalt has taken over and what's left is rubble trauma. Even after this empire system that we live in has fallen, the rubble will remain along with all the excess. That is sad and scary. *Dawn of the Matmosphere.*

BLACK BLOOD

The animation of concrete and asphalt and the black blood substance that we feed on, that we drink during the performances, we offer to the congregation, the Cultists, what looks like gloopy tar in the dark... it's actually some *spirulina*—a species of hi-tech bacteria that *produces its own food*—NASA wants to cultivate it in space. It's like a dark heavy green pigment powder stinking of algae and pond water, producing this chunky, gooey consistency when you mix it with liquids. Ancient Aztecs used to eat it. Supposedly, this is the original food-source that the first microscopic organisms consumed back when our early ancestors were cooking primordial soup. Even just a tiny portion is *full* of proteins, vitamins, and minerals—so it gives you this mad energy buzz as well, keeps you going for that whole hour while you're doing the ritual. And you can obviously spit it on each other and offer it to the crowd. It becomes a binder.

MOZIZIZM, MOZIZIZM

Chants and mantras are the content that creates a cult, forming the sonic landscape for followers to immerse and inhabit.

MOZIZIZM works both ways. Record yourself saying *MOZIZIZM* right now; do it in a deep slow voice, then play it backwards. It's a fucking *race-car.* Sampling has always played a big part in Hip-hop culture, and this rolls over into the way that our mantras and chants are born. There'll be an interesting lyric in a rap song, or a writer will say something in an interview—we sample that, slow it down, cut it up, break it down to the basic elements, and remix it again into this obsessive mutation of the original phrase. These are *'broken down Hip-hop ritual'*—the best advice that we give to our followers is "Don't complicate your life, *Cultiplicate* your life!" Look out in the future for pocket-sized Cult *Mantra Chanters* for the busy *Cultist* who needs to *brain wash n go.*

That's the thing—the sonic side of it is the nasal, obviously the Rammellzee's signature nasal style. So you know *Beastie Boys, Cypress Hill, Clouddead...* and that characterization that's the transformative *Rammellzeeness* of becoming nasal. We made a film called *the Sub-nasal Chamber.* In the film, how we package it, there's a Tarot Reader for a group of elite exo-conscious Cultistes, and when the Reader plays a card or gives us a selection, it jumps to a ritual from that card. Basically, within that fiction there's the Major Nasal Groove, which is like a higher cult level, and then there's the Minor Nasal Groove, which is subcultural paralysis.

This nods at the polarization of positive and negative with the Rammellzee's own mythologies. We also *reversed* the process of a traditional Tarot reading—embarking on our pilgrimage from the Westway to the Autobahn and everywhere in-between *before* the cards determined all of that. This is a massive victory in the battle against chronologics, as the forward passage of time is just another piece of the prison structure designed to limit our exo-conscious potential—and *that* is Major Nasal; *that* is how you achieve *anamnesis.*

JUNK

The Cult has a studio full of this junk piling up and looking trashy, but it holds energy within the performance. Suddenly, you can rechannel it. Reanimate the junk, reconfiguring into exoskeletons in the *cannon* of the Rammellzee art practice, until you're just a huge fucking plastic mass. It's that viral fever effect.   S k i p diving sub-cults; thrive on discarded plastics. Fanatics of the Three Stripes of ZI~DADA rip out sneaker souls and create trainer talismans and sabers, for channeling the plasmatic flow. When you actually walk down the street in a set of heavy ski-boots with something that looks like a giant lazer blaster over your shoulder and all this armor, rad shin-pads up and down your arms and legs, maybe a cloak, a visor—to a kid who just jumped off the bus, you look like a super alien manga action blaster, and it blows their mind! They get excited, they get inspired, they literally start poppin'. So it takes on this new life. It's ephemeral; but then, again, it's cargo cult—all life is a process of eternal regurgitation; it washes back, and you reingest it. It's obsessive.

In 2012 The Cult first performed a breakspray ritual under the Westway, paying homage to the first NY graffiti piece in London (by Futura 2000) leading to further street incursions such as a walking dead tour of the Heygate Estate and a breakdancing battle with rival cult Terminus 5 at Slough Bus station. In 2013 they exhibited at International Film Festival Rotterdam, Art Gallery Walsall and completed a residency at Hack The Barbican, including a climatic joint ritual with The House of Sequana and infamous freestyle battle rap champion Infinite Livez. In 2014 new members were initiated at Teufelsberg, an abandoned Berlin spy-station, and an Edinburgh observatory in the vicinity of the Athenian acropolis on Calton hill. The Cult was then infiltrated by The Dysonic Hoover Boyz during a Feral Expressway trail of destruction through an architectural model of the Oval area at the Gasworks artist run gallery in London. In order to mark the passing of the Rammellzee on the 27th June a lavish feast was held at The Pumphouse, a squatted museum in London, in collaboration with UK graffiti legend Petro who designed an 18 foot galactic banqueting table.

THE TICKET THAT IMPLODED— IN THE (ELECTRO)MAGNETIC INTERSTICE
Laurent Schmid

THE RABBIT HOLE

When Filippo Marinetti claimed that "Time and Space died yesterday" in the Futurist manifesto appearing in *Le Figaro* on February 20, 1909, they had already been dead for nearly fifty years. At first, the impact of the space-destroying effect that went hand in hand with the development of technology had been perceived physically, for the most part. Brought about by the railroad, this initial shock was profound. And when the second wave hit the masses in the form of the audio media, the impact was similarly drastic. The invention of the telephone and later the radio irrevocably changed space-time. After Philipp Reis introduced a prototype of his telephone to the public in Frankfurt in 1861 and explained it in his lecture "On the Reproduction of Tones at Any Desired Distance by Means of the Galvanic Current," the relationship between the body and space was no longer as clearly determinable as it had been before. Marinetti, of course, was referring primarily to the physical-mechanical negotiation of distances in a short time—a new phenomenon back then, which served to shrink those distances. The changes brought about by the media, however, encompassed a further aspect. Not only had it become possible to experience space in a different way physically; now it was even possible to detach a certain part of the body—the voice—and transport it into other spheres. An immaterial part of the self could be taken to a far distant place virtually the instant it came into being.

PINK ELEPHANTS ON PARADE

The experience of this separation bordered on magic, while at the same time outclassing everything the art of magic was capable of. It was also accordingly difficult to accept. Houdini, who had always spoken out against a spiritualist understanding of the magical arts and sought to communicate magic as a rational art of deception, had an entire elephant disappear before an audience—but without questioning or redefining the existing conception of space. The animal remained in the same space, simply concealed from the audience by a black cloth. *The elephant was in the room.* The fact that we are surrounded by things we cannot perceive was, in and of itself, nothing fundamentally new. Already more than a hundred years earlier, William Herschel and Johann Wilhelm Ritter had known about tones in frequencies we are not yet or no longer capable of hearing and light in wavelengths that do not correspond to our eyes. The discovery of further forms of electromagnetic waves, for example X-rays and radioactivity (both not so very long before Marinetti's manifesto), had made it clear that there are realms of our world that are accessible only with technical aids.
Heinrich Hertz first succeeded in transmitting and receiving electromagnetic waves —that is, waves consisting of interacting electric and magnetic fields—in

1886. In so doing, he confirmed James Clerk Maxwell's electromagnetic theory and laid the foundation for the concept that later led to the actual separation of message and sender, signal and body. The new, invisible and immaterial space thus formed had not been conceivable before the new inventions. Now, however, it was experienceable, accessible from different sides and at different times.   And incidentally: waves do not adhere to the idea of an environment surrounding the subject, but make radically clear that we ourselves are a part of space. The fact that waves and particles travel through us means that we are not only recipients of information, but at the same time a part of the ether. A mini Copernican revolution. Victor Franz Hess discovered cosmic radiation during a balloon ride in 1912 and wrote about it in: *Physikalische Zeitschrift,* vol. 13, Leipzig, Verlag S. Hirzel, 1912, p. 1084.

A few years later, in collaboration with Pino Masnata, F. T. Marinetti wrote his "La Radia" manifesto (appearing in the *Gazetta del Popolo* in 1933) dedicated to radio— "LA RADIA, the name that we futurists give to the great manifestations of the radio..."—once again formulating decisive observations on space:

"LA RADIA abolishes

1)   the space...
2)   time
3)   unity of action
4)   dramatic character
5)   the audience as self-appointed judging mass...

3)   The immensification of space. No longer visible and framable, the stage becomes universal and cosmic

4)   The reception amplification and transfiguration of vibrations emitted by living beings living or dead spirits dramas of wordless noise-states

5)   The reception amplification and transfiguration of vibrations emitted by matter. Just as today we listen to the song of the forest and the sea so tomorrow shall we be seduced by the vibrations of a diamond or a flower

6)   A pure organism of radio sensations

7)   An art without time or space without yesterday or tomorrow. The possibility of receiving broadcast stations situated in various time zones and the lack of light will destroy the hours of the day and night. The reception and amplification of the light and the voices of the past with thermoionic valves will destroy time

8)   The synthesis of infinite simultaneous actions ..."
       http://www.kunstradio.at/2002A/27_01_02/laradia-e.html
       (last accessed August 18, 2014).

This space is formed by the listener's imagination—or by the collective imagination of all listeners—and is not compelled to adhere to any topographical or architectonic situation. It exhibits the potential to contradict logical, rational, and objectively measurable facts. It is capable of creating a temporality all its own, in which the radiophonic conception and the transmitted material create a fluid, quasi anti-Hegelian space-time. In "Towards a Philosophy of

Sound Art," Salomé Voegelin points to the fact that commercial radio avoids this situation and does not function in this manner. "It does not use the potential of its own medium to question objective time, but paralyzes temporality in its strict schedule. It creates an über-objective time, the time all clocks can measure themselves by, and it demands of our body to bow its timetable. And it does not respond to the spatiality of its own medium either, which has the potential to create a possible world rather than insist on relaying what we see." In Salomé Voegelin, *Listening to Noise and Silence: Towards a Philosophy of Sound Art*, New York, Continuum, 2010. This non-space of radio exists simultaneously in my kitchen and in my car. But also in the homes of people I don't know. The quality of being everywhere is at the same time a quality of being nowhere. And nevertheless it is capable of creating ties, facilitating common experiences, and uniting the private and collective realms. One aspect of this simultaneity—the reception by multiple parties in the same instant—was initially described by Marconi as a problem: anyone who wanted to could receive his broadcasts. Artists such as Guillaume Apollinaire, Boccioni, Carrà, Delaunay, and Marinetti, however, recognizing the potential that lay in this circumstance, developed "Simultaneism" around 1913. The wireless transmission of voices not only points to invisible forces and interrelationships in our universe, to realms that evidently exist alongside the directly experienceable world. As early as the seventeenth century, scholars such as Athanasius Kircher recognized that there are such forces as magnetism binding the world together in "secret knots." It is to Kircher—who hardly distinguished between the directly experienceable and the indirectly experienceable universe—that we owe the term "electromagnetism." Athanasius Kircher, *Magnes sive de arte magnetica opus tripartitum*, Coloniae Agrippinae,

Apud Jodocum Kalcoven, 1643, p. 640. What is more, in the same work he discussed an unexpected link with language. Fascinated by the invisible force of magnetism, he went a step further and fantasized about the development of a "Machina Cryptologica," a kind of magnetic telegraph. In a later book devoted to linguistic theory and cryptography, he even went so far as to promise in the first two chapters: Athanasius Kircher and Lazzari Varese, *Polygraphia nova et universalis ex combinatoria arte detecta : Quàquiuis etiam linguarum quantumuis imperitus triplici methodo prima, vera & reali, sine ulla latentis arcani suspicione, manifestè*; secunda, per technologiam quondam..., Romae, Ex typographia Varesij, 1663. Also see Haun Saussy, "Magnetic Language, Athanasius Kircher and Communication." In Athanasius Kircher: *The Last Man Who Knew Everything*, New York, Routledge, 2004, p. 263.

Section I: The Reduction of All Languages to One. Section II: The Extension of One Language to All.

ANEWTHOUGHT MUST COME OUT IN A NEW LANGUAGE.— JACK SMITH Jack Smith in an interview with Sylvère Lotringer: "Uncle Fishook and the Sacred Baby Poo Poo of Art." In *Semiotexte*, vol. III, no. 2, 1978, p. 195; reprinted in Sylvère Lotringer, *Schizo-Culture: The Event, the Book*, Los Angeles, Semiotexte[e], 2013. In the same interview, on page 198: Sylvère Lotringer: "That's why Burroughs uses cut-ups: to try to prevent words from being twisted around." Jack Smith: "Oh, that's one way."

Marinetti, likewise, progressed in his manifestoes from space created with rays to linguistic space and availed himself of means already employed previously by Velimir Khlebnikov and the Russian Cubo-Futurists. New space is created by fragmentation of language, redefinition of syntax and language patterns, the formation of neologisms, etc. For Filippo Tommaso Marinetti, who coined the term "wireless imagination" (in his manifesto of May 11, 1913: "Destruction of Syntax—Wireless Imagination—Words-in-Freedom" / "Distruzione della sintassi—immaginazione senza fili—parole in libertà"), this not only included the collapse of syntax and the free interpretation of orthography, but went a step further than his "parole in libertà." The unbelievable speed also brought about the breakup of traditional structures and conventions and thus the formation and definition of fundamentally new types of connections. At about the same time, under the title "Lettre Océan," Guillaume Apollinaire published poems written in "liberated words" he referred to as "ideograms" or "calligrams" in the magazine *Soirées de Paris*, which he directed. In collaboration with Aleksei Kruchenykh (with whom he, Mikhail Matyushin, and Kasimir Malevich realized the first Futurist opera, *Victory over the Sun*), Khlebnikov even developed a new language: "Zaum." It was to be a universal language, a language of the stars or of the birds. The name "Zaum" ("за-ум") is ambiguous: idiomatically it means "nonsense," but it can also be understood as "located behind the mind, transmental." Language is always ideology and defined by value systems. A violation of the boundaries of conventional language is thus always a violation of fundamental orders and viewpoints. The negation of the norm, the bursting of the bounds of language, is always also an avowal of opposition. Differences in language point to differences in value systems. Half a century later, within the context of the counterculture movement in the U.S. and Europe, these tactics were once again widely employed.

Among other things, they were an important aspect of Radio Alice, which after the events of March 1977 had become a symbol of free radio: As Klemens Gruber demonstrates in his *Die zerstreute Avantgarde: strategische Kommunikation im Italien der 70er Jahre*, Vienna, Böhlau, 2010, p. 98. "Poliziotti, magistrati, giornalisti hanno detto che Radio Alice è oscena." Franco Berardi, *Alice è il diavolo: storia di una radio sovversiva*, Milan, Shake edizioni underground, 2001, p. 47. The collective A/traverso was initially surprised by this accusation, but then assimilated it— "Language, when it is freed from the sublimations which reduce it to the code and makes desire and the body speak, is obscene (literally: obscene)" Hedi Kholti, *Autonomia: Post-Political Politics*, 2nd ed., Los Angeles, CA, Semiotext[e], 2007, p. 131. —and its opponents referred to the language of Radio Alice as "creative-demenziale." Ugo Volli later called it "Demenziali-creative come Radio Alice di Bologna." In "Mode, modi, modelli," in Ernesto Galli Della Loggia. [u.a.] *Il trionfo del privato*, Rome-Bari, editori Laterza, 1980, p. 151. The qualities that distinguished the political hopes of the Autonomia movement were mirrored on the level of language: it was experimental and imaginative, rhizomatically organized, and equipped with a dash of humor.

Radio Alice frequently made explicit reference to Dada, and thus to sound poetry and collage, and also exhibited an undeniable affinity with Futurism. Visually in Radio Alice's leaflets or in their flyer of 1976 "Abasso la vostra morale. Abasso la vostra religione. Abasso la vostra politica. Abasso la vostra arte." In Franco Berardi and Gary Genosko, *After the Future*, Edinburgh, AK Press, 2011. Franco Bifo Berardi points out the common belief in the concept of the future. It should be recalled in this context that, already in the early twentieth century, a number of methods and linguistic attributes were making the rounds among the different artistic and literary currents. Raoul Hausmann, in his text on the history of the sound poem (1910—39), mentioned that Kandinsky had been familiar with Khlebnikov's "inventions" and had also had phonemes by Khlebnikov recited at the Cabaret Voltaire in Zürich in 1916 in the presence of Hugo Ball. Raoul Hausmann, "Zur Geschichte des Lautgedichts." In *Am Anfang war Dada*, Steinbach/Giessen, Anabas-Verlag G. Kämpf, 1972; reprinted in 1992, pp. 35—47. Since then, and after the success of Kurt Schwitter's Ursonate in the twenties, there were several parallel forms developed on these roots, as the lettrism in France and also later movements of sound poetry or abstract poetry often giving preference to tape recorder to capture it.

A MIRROR

The technology of sound recording—likewise developed in the 1880s—contributed yet another aspect to the detachment of the voice from the body and its subsequent multiplication in that context. With the aid of a method based on magnetism, the experience of time in its entirety was redefined. Voices, which had been considered an inseparable part of the human body until the advent of radio technology, could now be stored and played back at a later time. Because of the fact that radio and sound recording shared certain characteristics—both were based on electromagnetism and both detached the voice from the body—they were considered related media. After the advent of mechanical gramophone techniques, a recording device based on magnetization was introduced by the Danish engineer Valdemar Poulsen at the Paris World Fair of 1900. Marconi had also been involved in the development of this method, which came into wide use in the 1930s. Both G. Marconi and T. A. Edison evidently believed in the possibility of making contact with deceased persons with the aid of telepathy. (http://news.bbc.co.uk/2/hi/uk_news/magazine/4185356.stm, accessed on 19 August 2014).

In the 1950s, the opera singer Friedrich Jürgenson recorded singing chaffinches outside Stockholm. When he played the recordings, he heard strange voices he had not noticed during the recording process. He and Konstantīns Raudive developed the technique of telepathic voice recording, thus making further advances into the world created by this technology. Jürgenson accordingly called his book Voices from Space (1964). Raudive spent much of the last ten years of his life exploring EVP (electronic voice phenomena). With the help of various electronics experts, he recorded over 100,000 audiotapes, most of which were made under what he described as "strict laboratory conditions." He occasionally collaborated with Bender. Over four hundred people were involved in his research, and all of them apparently heard the voices. This culminated in the 1968 publication of Unhörbares wird hörbar ("What is inaudible becomes audible"). Friedrich Jürgenson, Rösterna från rymden, Stockholm, Saxon & Lindström,1964. Konstantīns Raudive, Breakthrough: An Amazing Experiment in Electronic Communication with the Dead, New York, Taplinger, 1971. Since they knew that the voice could be separated from the body and heard at a later time, they were convinced that they were entering a realm where they could hear the voices of the dead. Both Jürgenson and Raudive were certain that these voices did not proceed from randomly recorded radio signals. It was theorized that sounds could take on illusory qualities when they were repeated. The British psychologist Richard M. Warren dubbed the process by which unintelligible sounds supposedly evolved back into meaningful words "the verbal transformation effect." For Raudive, fragments others described as "glubbo," "buduloo," or "vum vum" actually formed the word "Lenin." In one of

Elli's experiments described by Roach on p. 187: Mary Roach, *Spook: Science Tackles* the Afterlife, New York: W. W. Norton, 2005.

These investigations influenced artists like Öyvind Fahlström who created hybrid bird-human languages like "Birdo" or "Whammo, based on similar sounds he developed during a stay in New York for his two radio plays 'Fåglar I Sverige' and 'Den heilige Thorsten Nillsson'. The idea of creating a major work came with the tape recorder he was given by his wife, Barbro Östlihn. In a postcard he wrote to Billy Klüver in 1965: "Working on 'The Holy Torsten Nilsson', all my film sound tapes, and a Nova-type story about Sweden' Undated postcard from Fahlströhm, in Billy Klüver's archive, in: Teddy Hultberg, *Öyvind Fahlström on the Air—Manipulating the World*, Stockholm, Sveriges Radio förlag, 1999. The tapes he was referring were his recordings of film soundtracks he recorded himself mostly from his TV in New York. The 'Nova' reference is to William Borroughs' cut-up novel "Nova Express".

WONDER-
LAND

Genesis P-Orridge, in search of affinities and similarities between art and magic, found his way to William S. Burroughs and Brion Gysin. In the early 1980s (the period in which P-Orridge and Peter Christopherson founded *Psychic TV* and the *Temple of Psychic Youth*) the three of them experimented with recording the voices of dead people on magnetic tape without a microphone. Taking Konstantīns Raudive's theories as a point of departure, they proceeded on the assumption of a hypothetical link between spoken language and the world. William S. Burroughs, Electronic Revolution, 2nd enl. ed. by Feedback from Watergate to the Garden of Eden, S.I.: Expanded Media Editions, 1976.   Burroughs had already been working with Raudive's technique for quite some time. Entirely in keeping with the ideas of anti-psychiatry and schizoanalysis, he argued that this method disproved "the whole psychiatric dogma that voices are the imagination of a sick mind." William Burroughs, "It belongs to the Cucumbers." In The Adding Machine, New York, Seaver Books, 1986, p. 59.   Since Gysin and Burroughs had already come to conceive of recording tape as a magical tool in connection with their use of the cut-up technique, these experiments did not represent anything fundamentally new in their work. Genesis P-Orridge recalled: "What Bill explained to me then was pivotal to the unfolding of my life and art. Everything is recorded. If it is recorded, then it can be edited. If it can be edited, then the order, sense, meaning and direction are as arbitrary and personal as the agenda and/or person editing. This is magick [sic]."Genesis P-Orridge, "The Magical Processes and Methods of William S. Burroughs and Brion Gysin." In Richard Metzger, Book of Lies: The Disinformation Guide to Magick and the Occult, New York, NY, Disinformation Co., 2003, p. 106. There was no doubt in their minds about the relationship between technology and the occult: "Burroughs and Gysin both told me something that resonated with me for the rest of my life so far. They pointed out that alchemists always used the most modern equipment and mathematics, the most precise science of their day." Idem, p. 113.   Gysin's use of the cut-up technique—a concept that can be traced to the Dadaist writer Tristan Tzara—had initially been confined to paper. He and Burroughs then expanded on it by fragmenting and rearranging words on magnetic tape. Burroughs was convinced that, on the level of text, the true meanings behind words could be discovered and the time barrier no longer applied: "When you cut into the present the future leaks out." Cf. "Origin and Theory of the Cut-Ups", the recording of a lecture delivered in 1967 at Naropa University in Boulder, on the LP Break Through in Grey Room. William S. Burroughs, Break Through in Grey Room, Vienna and Munich, Sub Rosa, 2001. For Burroughs, it followed that reality could be modified with the audio cut-up method. Without batting an eyelash, P-Orridge referred to this as "altering reality." Since, as Burroughs insisted, everything had already been recorded, it was entirely possible to make changes.

The influence of Gysin and Burroughs was initially limited to a small group of artists, musicians, and writers. In addition to biographical and personal aspects, they apparently also shared certain conceptions of space-time and the effect of language. The city of Tangier—the "Interzone" in which they had gathered—moreover gave them a sense of being exempt from the conventions and constraints of society.

The group comprised various counterculture legends such as Ira Cohen—who in collaboration with the Living Theatre members Mel Clay and Petra Vogt had also experimented with cut-ups—and Angus and Hetty MacLise. They had arrived at spoken language from a wide range of media: Cohen from photography and film, Vogt from the theater, MacLise from music. What they had in common, however, was their interest in the voice, the relationship between the world and the body, the meaning of the (mass) media, and the word as a tool of illusion and control. They were strongly influenced by Burroughs's language theories: he proceeded on the assumption of a system that functioned in like manner in ancient cultures and modern society. The "disembodied voices"—of priests or the mass media, depending on the context—infiltrated the individual and occupied his brain.

OFF SCENE

By the time of his death, Félix Guattari had not found time to set forth his promising ideas about creative and political resistance and what he called the liberated, "resingularized" subjectivity of the post-media era in any detail. Félix Guattari and Sylvère Lotringer, *Chaosophy: Soft Subversions*, New York, N.Y., Semiotext[e], 1996. Yet even his sketchy notes on the subject point in the direction of an anti-hierarchical, anti-representative structure in what is meanwhile an entirely new media situation, a structure whose fragmentary quality serves to liberate it from authoritarian forces.

As strategies for resistance, the fragmentation and reassembly of existing linguistic forms and invention of new ones do indeed appear to be among the very few remaining tactics for efficiently opposing new forms of (mass) media control.

How do I know what and how much information about me is floating around in the data clouds, where it comes from, how up to date, and how correct it is? Ultimately, my only way of preserving and protecting my privacy and identity is to create parallel identities and apply the above-described imaginative techniques of language destruction and reinvention. Neologisms, fragmentation, and multiplication can help me restore my freedom and uniqueness in this realm. Algorithms have no sense of humor and don't know how to deal with inventiveness. In the world of data, fantasized parallel worlds protect my freedom on a physically experienceable level. Even if Internet radio has substantially simplified access to radio and is thus very democratic in nature, it is located on terrain that is subject to a dangerous degree of control. Everything can be retraced; a lot is stored. How would Bertolt Brecht have reacted to this situation—a man who once dreamed not only of producing and broadcasting radio, but also of recording everything? Likewise in the area of metadata, even the smallest web radio can reveal a great amount of information about ourselves. Every listener can be identified and traced; his consumer behavior can be analyzed, patterns be looked for in it, and linguistic analyses carried out. It is all completely exposed and there for the construal. The precision of the name of the free radio station *Alice*, in which Guattari was involved for a time, is nothing short of amazing. It makes reference not only to a fantastic tale in which the space-time continuum is thrown into complete disarray, but also to the author, Lewis Carroll, who in the sequel *Through the Looking Glass* of 1871, published *Jabberwocky*, a nonsense poem that—discovered by Alice in a book in the parallel world behind the mirror—uses neologisms and nonsense words to dissolve linguistic structure.

FILM-POEMS FOR THE ARTIST-RADIO
Quinn Latimer

In the summer of 2013, inside the gated garden/driveway of the Maison Baron in Geneva, on Rue Subilia 45, I delivered a talk and reading to a gathering of participants of LapTopRadio's "Wonderlust" about a series of texts I was then working on. The texts are called "Twenty Film-Poems for M. Auder." They were and are a series of mini-essays on selected videos by Michel Auder, the French-born, New York-based experimental filmmaker. Each individual text takes its title from one Auder video; then I proceeded to elliptically transcribe it into language—its ideas, images, media, montages, sounds, meanings, suggestions. The texts are strange, inverted hybrids: instead of writing a script and then making a movie from it, they take script-less videos as their starting point and then attempt to discursively transcribe them into a form at once essayistic and poetic, academic and casual. In this way, I thought them pertinent to the idea of LapTopRadio itself, in which a series of artists—who usually work in "visual" art forms—create sonic or textual works to be broadcast without visuals. It's an instructive inversion. Here's another one: my series of texts about Michel Auder has now been published in *Stories, Myths, Ironies, and Other Songs: Conceived, Directed, Edited, and Produced by M. Auder* Stories, Myths, Ironies, and Other Songs: Conceived, Directed, Edited, and Produced by M. Auder, Berlin, Sternberg Press, 2014., a monograph, and catalogue raisonné of Auder's moving image works. But how do you show films—so many moving images—inside the static pages of a book? It's a question, isn't it. Likewise: how do you listen to visual art? That's another question. Here are some more.

Excerpts from "Twenty Film-Poems for M. Auder"

ROMAN VARIATIONS (1991)

Rome. The video unfolds. Fragments of rose-hued skies, fuzzy Italian television programs, street protests, tourist-strewn cathedrals, views from a window. The filmmaker's camera roves inquisitively over church frescoes and religious paintings, pausing quietly at images of sex and/or violence: John the Baptist's severed head. See his look, its severe disquiet. Before, on the plane, there a woman files her nails—her hands illuminated, as if in a religious painting, as if on fire, by the plane's overhead light—then plays with her diamond ring, then takes some pills. Files spill like water from her purse. The small orange pill bottle like an omen, like a mouth. There, in Rome, an old woman washes clothes along the low stone steps of a river; the steps enter the water like a drinking body. Is she crying or singing? An ambulance screams past. Boys in jeans jackets push their Vespas up the pale, steep steps to the street. Engines also screaming, a kind of music. Skies pale then red as a mouth. Walls bleaching then blushing orange (memories of pills, mouths that would receive them). Windows as dark and brooding as—what?—eyes. Not screens. The song keeps changing on the radio. The doctor on Italian TV looks like a priest. His patient, in her black bra and gold necklace, smiles and nods her small, dark head. He listens to her heart, speaks paternalistically. He taps her chest with his small, dark hammer. The channel changes. The tone conjured—reticent, evocative, dryly luminescent, as the filmmaker considers city, history, self—is somewhat Sebaldian. That kind of fiction, that kind of document, that kind of negative, illumined excursus. If W. G. Sebald had liked Italian television medical dramas, liked filmic fragments—had made a film, even—it might look very much like this one, says the critic. "I have always believed that I am closer to literature and writing than to cinema," says M. Auder.

CHRONICLES MOROCCO (1971—72)

"I hate traveling and explorers," writes that traveler, that explorer, Claude Lévi-Strauss. "Nowadays, being an explorer is a trade, which consists not, as one might think, in discovering hitherto unknown facts after years of study, but in covering a great many miles and assembling lantern-slides or motion pictures, preferably in color, so as to fill a hall with an audience for several days in succession." Some twenty years later, another Frenchman begins a journey, covering some miles, assembling some images. He goes to Morocco, where he makes motion pictures of his travels. His journey is a family vacation, however, not an anthropological research trip; his palette is black and white, not color. He has no hall, no audience; this is M. Auder. He has images: a boy aiming a gun at him, smiling, through a small hole in a clay wall that encircles the city, that bazaar. Camels crossing a beach. Old men traversing roads on donkeys, their thin faces like dark stems under the bright-white petals of fabric that bloom from their heads. Their turbans like signs, like language, like flowers. Children gather around a car. M. Auder's own hand, reaching from the bottom of the frame to its center, into another frame—his van's open window—to offer some coins to a reaching child. The filmmaker's wife and child, smiling briefly, blankly, and gone. The flat white roofs of a town, baking like bright white screens—absent any films—in the sun. Dunes and stretches of beach, baking in the bright white projection of the sun. Everything is a film. Everything is an image. Village, caravan, wall, eggs, hashish, ocean, European, Moroccan, Bedouin, American. Seagulls strobing the sky with their white and dark. We, the viewer, stand in the shade of (the relevant) literature for a second. It is cooler here. Paul and Jane Bowles, Susan Sontag, Tennessee Williams, W. G. Sebald, and Levi-Strauss himself offer us some spectral water, their words, those luminous and shaded literary travelogues. Then they take them away. They grin, dryly, and disappear; they were never here. ("Linguistic proximity and duplicitous deterritorialization go together in the cinematic enterprise," says Marie-Claire Ropars.) We are in the sun again, under the glare of M. Auder, his long, white stare. We blink and try to make out the images. The film burns, like the sun. The sun burns, like a film.

STORIES, MYTHS, IRONIES, AND SONGS
(1983)

Winter. Story needs a form. Narrative needs a. Name some forms. Myth, irony, song. Winter can be a form, too. See what happens inside its structure: a couple in bed under the covers; a figure hunched over in a blizzard. A white street, dark window. The stories on both sides of it; stories in chapters. I'll sing you a song about the battle between me and my nature, goes Ned Sublette over the moving images. Forward goes M. Auder's video. What's an anthology? What's a season? What's he doing? Disaster, weather, violence, weather, singing, weather, dictator, weather, television. Everything happens on a monitor. Hitler, Goebbels, the latter the former's minister of propaganda. His dead niece, his dead children. But Europe is over. On to the animal kingdom, its horses, its races, its nuns and priests and televised blessings. Anointing the animals, then hurtling them around the coliseum. Riders fall, horses fall. Some strange, technological font falls and reads: BEHAVIOR CHANGES BECAUSE OF ITS CONSEQUENCES. Horse clop and dismay through the blue frame: MASTURBATION. The chapter changes. Text scrolls across the monitor. A man with long hair tells the story of his adolescent evenings under the covers, controlling his "breathing." The man calls masturbation "breathing." His voice too sweet, too passive, as though he had been hurt as a child or thinks his breathiness attractive. Images of fashion models and pornography, open mouths and diamond rings, four-color printing. A kind of Cold War image culture, its specific advertorial vernacular. "In his essay 'Subversive Signs,' Hal Foster remarks that the appropriation artist (visual) is a 'manipulator of signs more than a producer of art objects, and the viewer an active reader of messages rather than a passive contemplator of the aesthetic or consumer of the spectacle,'" write Vanessa Place and Robert Fitterman. "'To read what was never written.' Such reading is the most ancient: reading before all languages, from the entrails, the stars, or dances," maintains Walter Benjamin. Note that each quote appropriates (manipulates) others. As M. Auder does. As does this critic, too. Theft, that handling, is also a kind of form. See how it fences in the caught. "The critique is in the reframing. The critique of the critique is in the echoing," Place and Fitterman echo.

EDGERYDERS   Nadia EL-Imam

"When is art relevant?" I asked a hall full of students and staff at art faculties, artists, arts institution representatives, journalists, politicians, etc.

For me, art is relevant when it allies itself with some societal forces. They can be the forces of conservation or those of change. Conservation as in Michelangelo or Bach. Change as in the Futurists or Beethoven (symphony, Napoleon winds of change).

Change is happening now at the edges. With what Edgeryders, the community and organization I co-founded, does and what countless others do. The Convincing thing is that this is happening anyway. The people in lead are scientists, data analysts, hackers, engineers, activists. Not nearly enough artists, though, because doing so is to go against the way interests in the art world are aligned in places where we still have the legacy of state-funded art. If you know what's good for you, will follow that very particular track. You won't have time to go to hacker unConferences or experiment with cryptography.

There is, however, clearly a need for art in this space, so much so that the unMonastery is going past sharing space by deploying cultural artifacts borrowed from the monastic orders, whether it be ritual, language, or garments. Aesthetics are important in signaling that we're doing something different. So one could argue you could increase the impact of artists in accompanying or facilitating societal change by encouraging them from a funding point of view to do this stuff. However, it requires rethinking what art projects are and who is an artist. Yes, there will be casualties and mistakes, but that is inevitable when you are trying to do something new.

But let me go back in time and tell you a story.

In the sixth century, a noble Roman called Benedict from Mursia fled the empire's capital, disgusted by its corruption. He founded a monastery based on communal life, prayer, and work as an ennobling activity.

As social innovations go, this was a major hit; it developed incredibly important innovations, such as the scriptoria to copy manuscripts and preserve ancient knowledge as the Roman Empire burned down.

It had major societal impact, acting as the cultural backbone of Charlemagne's universal empire; it scaled really well, becoming global in the medieval Christendom context, with monasteries from Ireland all the way to Bohemia. It still exists today, proving extremely sustainable over fifteen centuries. All this with no central command. Just a protocol for monks to interact as they lived together in a monastery.

The unMonastery is a residency scheme for social innovators, hackers, makers, and generally people at the edge. It is more than an idea: Edgeryders been prototyping it in an ancient small city of Southern Italy called Matera for about a year now.

 What makes it unique is that it tries to redeploy in a lay, innovation-oriented way some of the practices that made medieval Western monasticism so successful.

Specifically, it is designed so that the unMonastery is explicitly at the service of the hosting local community. In Matera, we ran participatory workshops with local citizens to find out which challenges they face. And it is not modeled on the business corporation.

Not even the not-for-profit one. It tries to draw sustainability by producing things that are beautiful, clever, and useful to the local community. The idea is that the community, recognizing this, will support its unMonastery, not necessarily by donating money. unMonastery Matera receives donations in materials, electricity, and biscuits from a local biscuit manufacturer.

Many projects can happen in an unMonastery. In Matera, Elf is building a mesh network to share connectivity; Marc an open source solar tracker to increase the yield of solar panels; Lois is prototyping an online version of a farmers' market in collaboration with a German startup; Bembo is working hard on inventing new traditions that help unMonasterians to work as a group and the local citizens to interact smoothly with the unMonastery itself.

We are very proud of the unMonastery's openness: check out their open data website, where you can see not only how projects are progressing, but how much money they spend on food and what percentage of the food they buy is local and organic. Even their energy consumption in real time through a project we call Open Energy Monitor. And it's only one of the initiatives coming out of Edgeryders.

The unMonastery is an alternative response to exploding youth unemployment that came out of a discussion about the need to reconcile the need to make a living with the need to make meaning.  Where government and institutions' responses are to push young people to adapt to a labor market that is structurally flawed, by becoming more indebted or accepting ever-worsening conditions, we asked what needs are we trying to satisfy through a job, and are there other ways to fulfill them? Three needs.

If you have more diverse conversations, with people who have very different perspectives... different questions are asked... and different solutions proposed.

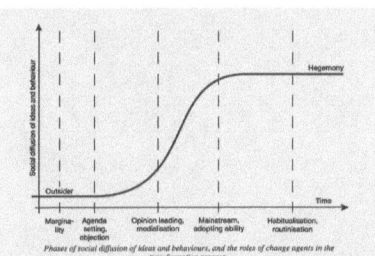

Phases of social diffusion of ideas and behaviours, and the roles of change agents in the transformation process.

Apparently, state-level actors want to include the unMonastery in a national development plan for rural areas and roll it out as a nationwide program. They are asking Edgeryders for help in shaping the policies. Not bad for a project that started out as an online conversation between a bunch of hackers, artists, and misfits in different parts of the world.

This techmonk movement is one of many interesting and relevant trends that are either initiated or visible very early on in Edgeryders. The advantage with working this way is that you see what others miss and build connections others cannot. Here, I would really like to show that the edges have always had their say—maybe a less dramatic example, but most things we are comfortable today with were once the edge stuff. Remember: the idea of one person having one vote was once a radical idea.

How can established actors work together with radical communities? For example, we can try to do foresight studies. And in doing so, contribute towards building the much needed infrastructure for the continent's civic hackers, makers, artists, innovators, and next generation leaders to come together with peers all over the world, inspire one another and help each other. P2P.

THE ETERNAL INTERNET BROTHERHOOD
Angelo Plessas

LAURENT SCHMID: What was the idea behind "The Eternal Internet Brotherhood?

ANGELO PLESSAS: The Eternal Internet Brotherhood started abstractly as an initiative for a gathering of different people whom I admired online. It was a chance for an internet hookup of my internet brothers and sisters materialized in a beautiful setting after a prior communication of Facebook likes, Twitter mentions, and Instagram following. It would combine work and holidays… some sort of residency but not in the conventional sense because there is not an institutional intent or aspiration, no support from anywhere, and it would always take place in a remote place. I was also interested to see what would be the outcome of a gathering like this. More specifically, I was intrigued by the idea how an artwork could be "produced" or evolved in a setting like this without existing in the comfort zone of our cities and our studios. At the same time, the financial situation in Greece speeded up the realization of this idea because many people here, especially in the art community, were very stressed with their lives. I started imagining of moving to India, living in an ashram, and initiating something there. Finally, after a series of events and requests, I decided to make this experience a reality for a few days every year, even though you never know it might be forever in the future. I brought together artists, writers, poets, curators, and architects in the perfection of nature; we created works on the spot but also became friends and shared pleasure. The Eternal Internet Brotherhood has already happened for three consecutive years in Greece, in Mexico, and in Israel/W. Bank. I am preparing the fourth edition in another extraordinary place next year. [note] Other events followed since 2014: http://eternalinternetbrotherhood.com

LS: Why did you start this project?

AP: We live in cities where capitalist, neo-liberal formations are being magnified, and consequently, culture is very much affected by it. I find cities more and more dystopian and the quality of life is deteriorating. All these "cool" metropolises, hangouts for rich hipsters, are being deserted by real artists or young creatives, and they are overrun by bankers and the rich. In the same manner, I have started to criticize the Internet, too, because it's becoming an aggressive expansion of this system. On the one hand, we have become providers of free labor for corporations, we sabotage our own privacy, and our attention is their biggest merchandise. On the other hand, it's becoming dehumanizing in social relations. We are becoming gradually distant, superficial, and even narcissistic. Everything is just so easily on your "plate," ready to be consumed and devoured. I don't see any rebellious imagination, and under this mindset, there is no quest for the unknown. Out of this context, I have become an obsessed topophile. Since I started doing the Brotherhood, I find myself reading only travel guides or looking into lost and forgotten places where we could go and find new inspirations. The Eternal Internet Brotherhood is all about that: free-yourself-start-browsing-the-physical-world-it-won't-be-there-forever.

LS: Could you describe its relation to technology? Is it a significant factor?

AP: Since the early 2000s, I have been part of a collective called Neen, which explores the emotional and poetic aspects of technology and the Internet. I never liked technology aesthetics. Most of the artworks using technology as a statement are gimmicky, didactic, and spiritless. The same applies to the Eternal Internet Brotherhood, where we are exploring new meanings and approaches regarding how the Internet can be viewed as a new situation, reversing the notion of an only-machine and -technological tool. I see the Brotherhood as an integrative format where we explore key issues echoing from the Internet, such as self-regulation, distribution, materiality, social interaction layered with mysticism, well-being, and ancient anthropology—especially to peripheries where the good traces of the Internet will act as an ideological tool. The ETINTERBRO is a situation for these kinds of reversals and contradictions, having no audience but being full of pleasures, smells, sounds, dreams, and lots of time to look at the stars.

LS: We could try to focus on some essential elements and clarify ideas and concepts of "The Eternal Internet Brotherhood" through a playful ping-pong. I give you a keyword, an image, a song title, and you answer with common elements of EIB.

LS: Let's start with some images:

Ira Cohen and Angus MacLise's Kathmandu-based publishing imprint.

AP:

Etinterbro Bird-Eye View

Logo, Angelo Plessas

LS:

Alighiero Boetti's One Hotel 1970's in Kabul,

AP:

Hippie bus,

LS:… and some keywords: Awareness
AP: Polytemporal Comfort, Pleasure of the Corporeal.
LS: Conviviality   AP: Interactive Matrix

of Human Interactions, Instinctive Synchronized Emotionalisms, Mindset Transfers, Silent Foreverness.

LS: Relational aesthetics   AP: Yoga and Relaxation Art, Gymnastic Art, Pranic Healing Art, Theme Park Art, Tea Ceremony Art, Ice Cream Art, Mud Art, Sand Art, Spiritual Wind Art, Water Art, Pareo Art, User-Customized Architecture, Robot Poetry

LS: Noosphere   AP: Post-Internet Improvisations, Manual Mental Fluidities, Extropic Optimisms.

LS: Sampling paradise.
AP: Invisible Demonstrations and Painting, Wet Projections and Lectures, Endurance Ultrasound Survivalism, Esoteric Spectacular Lasershows, Jackal Echo Lullabies, Palestinian Techno Jamming.

LS: De-schooling.   AP: Automated Freedom Performances, Software Craftsmanship Round Table, Live Streamed Meditation Sessions, Animal Sound Recordings, Horseback Riding Workshops, Remote Pranic Healing Symposium.

LS: Paleocybernetic age.   AP: Totem of the Post-Gender, The Tomb of Intellectual Property, The Kingdom of Develotopia, Emoji Catacombs, Monument to the Unknown Clicktivist, The Temple of Sharing, The Tower of Soft Power, Cave of the Selfie.

LS: Here we go with a couple of opposite positions: Red, green, blue: Harry Smith's alchemical schema representing the elements water, fire, and air vs. the three primary led-screen colors. Electric fields generated by electrically charged particles vs. electrical theology.

AP:

LS: Lenin's "electrical training of the masses"; the idea of electricity as a driving force behind socialism that he suggested during the Communist Party Congress of 1920 vs. power sources at Burning Man: Batteries, Solar Power, Wind, Biodiesel Generators.

AP:

LS: Pirate Utopia vs. Data Heaven. Crypto Anarchy vs. Friend-to-Friend.

AP:

 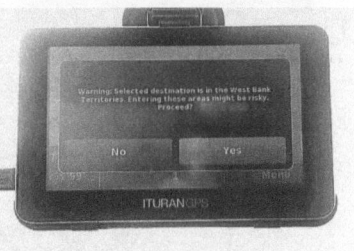

LS: Let me propose to you some sounds: Phill Niblock—Sweet Potato [Touch] https://www.youtube.com/watch?v=O-pJa2XoNCY

AP:

Pia Elcin Joyner, Daily Sunset Yoga Session. Dead Sea, 2014.

LS: **A.R. & Machines—Die Grüne Reise 1971** https://www.youtube.com/watch?v=AMsCOHp2_yM

AP:

The Media Ecosystem book by Antonio Lopez and an image by Joe Hamilton did in Las Pozas.

LS: Agitation Free—Malesch (1972) https://www.youtube.com/watch?v=iai7_F5nZyQ

AP:

The road signs by the roads on the Dead Sea, 2014.

LS: Alva Noto & Ryuichi Sakamoto Vrioon https://www.youtube.com/watch?v=IYeP8a_Y_0A

AP:

Internet on Board, going to Las Pozas, Mexico 2013.

LS: Angus MacLise & Tony Conrad—druid's leafy nest https://www.youtube.com/watch?v=q7Jy0voe3-w

AP:

Eternal HeadStand by Vincent Charlebois, Las Pozas, 2013.

LS: Date Palms—Yuba Reprise https://www.youtube.com/watch?v=T354gVbCy_c

AP:

Botanical Garden Kibbutz Circus by Anastasios Logo-thetis, at En Gedi, Dead Sea, 2014.

LS: Ghédalia Tazartès—Un Amour Si Grand Qu'il Nie Son Objet https://www.youtube.com/watch?v=nURr8ma2KWI

AP:

Just before the projection of Cibelle's piece, in Las Pozas, Mexico, 2013.

LS: Islas reso-nantes, Eliane Radigue https://www.youtube.com/watch?v=1RrsiGmLp_E

AP:

An Idea for Etinterbro Situation inspired by a model of Andreas Angelidakis, 2013.

LS: Join Inn—Ash Ra Tempel (1973) https://www.youtube.com/watch?v=-6_qZPjLyJA

AP:

Almost clubbing in Xilitla village, Xilitla near Las Pozas, 2013.

LS: **La Monte Young and Marian Zazeela—The Theatre of Eternal Music** https://www.youtube.com/watch?v=zlCg_2pK1oM

AP:

The Sacrifice by Joe Hamilton, in Las Pozas, 2013.

LS: Osamu Kitajima—Benzaiten 1974
https://www.youtube.com/watch?v=c87ARHzyO4k

AP:

VariousDisplays in Mexico, 2013.

LS: **Pauline**
Oliveros—**Mnemonics** III https://www.youtube.com/
watch?v=Msg4m8pzHoE

AP:

InAllOurMinds is the light,
Las Pozas, 2013.

LS: Psychic Ills—Mind Daze
https://www.youtube.com/watch?v=ugue9uLoHbU

AP:

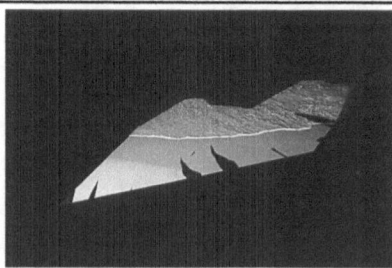 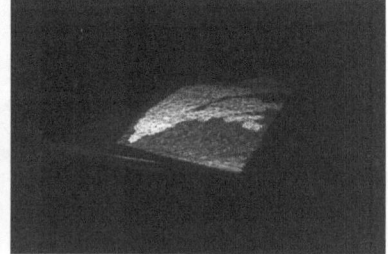

WetProjection by Priscilla Tea, Anafi, 2012.

LS: Yoko Ono with Thurston Moore & Kim Gordon—Mulberry (Live) https://www.youtube.com/watch?v=LlxKrgw-xgc

AP:

Tea Ceremony by Mai Ueda during the multi-live-streamed performance, Dead Sea, 2014.

THE KAFKA MACHINE: A THREE HOURS TESTAMENT
A PROJECT ON AUTONOMIA, ABSTRACT MACHINES, VOICES, & THE PRODUCTION OF SUBJECTIVITY

Willem van Weelden A project by DOGtime IDUM

Gerrit Rietveld Academie, Amsterdam. Jelmer Luyting, Alexander Schierl, Gosia Kaczmarek, Eugen Georg, Jefta Hoed, Willem van Weelden, 2012

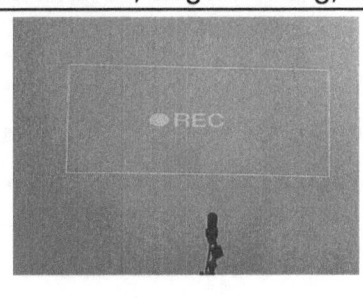 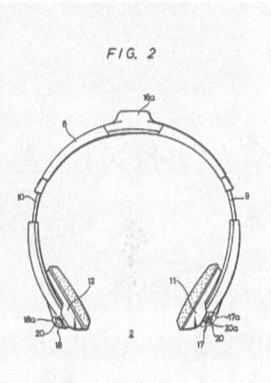

FIG. 2

Controller: All who are here today must remember that we are gathered in a ritual to approach what is called Kafka through Kafka, by Kafka, with Kafka.

Three: Whatever Kafka means. (She speaks, dreamily.)

Two: Kafka? Someone said Kafka... Kafka? (A sudden cry.)

Three: What is Kafka?

Controller: (Moving towards Three, threatening her with a knife). We are joined in a struggle against incomprehensible odds. We must all enter the ceremony.

'The dream reveals the reality which conception lags behind, that is the horror of life, the terror of art.'
                                          Franz Kafka

'The machine always depends on exterior elements in order to be able to exist as such. It implies a complementarity, not just with the man who fabricates it, makes it function or destroys it, but it is itself in a relation of alterity with other virtual or actual machines—a 'non-human' enunciation, a proto-subjective diagram.' From "Machinic Heterogenesis" Félix Guattari, 1992

THE KAFKA MACHINE: A MACHINIC DREAM

Kafka was Félix Guattari's favorite author, and throughout his career, he kept him close by. Not only did he envisage with Gilles Deleuze the concept of a minoritarian literature on the surface of the literary legacy of the Czech writer and insurance officer (trained as a lawyer), but in 1984, in the midst of what he called 'The Winter Years,' he contributed to 'a Kafka event' ('Le siècle de Kafka') at the Centre Pompidou in Paris. The exhibition, curated by Yasha David and assisted by Guattari, was a D&G assemblage that, on the occasion of his 100th anniversary, gave insight into a body of work sprung forth from the literary well that Kafka had broached. It was a theater of dreams, partly multimedial, theatrical, and cinematic in nature, but all of the installations, screenings, and seminars were in some sense touched by the dreamlike, nightmarish quality of Kafka's legacy. In the same context, Guattari in the course of conceiving a never-realized television project by Kafka ('Project for a Film by Kafka'), a project that had to be an embodiment of the affects brought about by Kafka's literary work as 'non-human becomings' passing through television, wrote about a selection of 65 dreams he found in the literary legacy of Kafka (in the journals and in his correspondence). These dreams were vital to the literary output of Kafka, as they were recognized by him as a mutating subjectivity, bearer of potentiality, susceptible to an endless enrichment of his literary hypnagogic imagination. For as Kafka wrote in one of his journals: life came to him as if in a dream. Guattari, psycho analyst in profession, was interested in the Kafka dreams in a way that exceeded the traditional dream analysis done in Freudian psycho analysis. He rejected the Freudian interpretative tradition of dreams ('Traumdeutung'), as he was more interested in how dreams in Kafka's work could ignite the process of the production of a collective subjectivity. He was more interested in the 'polyvocality' (the many-voiced-ness, to use the Bakhtinian term) of dreams and how these different voices would embody new gestures, reflexes, and refrains that at the same time would act defensively or aggressively, but in any way double and ambiguous, against the backdrop of a society falling victim to an ever-growing bureaucracy and invisible subjection. Guattari described them as 'open, machinic indices,' as they break open existing semiotic and behavioral chains. This image of a Kafka Machine as being an antidote to territorializing the effects of subjectivity and a refuge for a new emancipatory sensibility that springs forward out of Guattari's approach to Kafka, formed the inspiration for the project. The Kafkaen dreams are diverse in nature, at once grim, haunted, and menacing, and at other moments they are absurd and funny, or downright stupid. They form a literary desiring machine that produces micro-revolutions of a new subjectivity that in a polyphonic way can challenge our ear drums as voices that point to a future of dreamt actions.

The Kafka Machine, in the context of the project LRSN (La Radio Siamo Noi), is an evolving, interactive sound installation by students of the IDUM (Interaction Design Unstable Media) department of the DOGtime course at the Rietveld Academie Amsterdam and Willem van Weelden (mentor and tutor of that department). It is an experimental piece done to probe in a given interactive/curatorial environment the use of sounds as a dramaturgy to deliver an exposé with five 'testaments / legacies' that are related to the theme of the LRSN project. As LRSN points to the Autonomia movement and the use of radio as a media tactical weapon of alternative subjectivation, the project has given itself the task to investigate and work on five legacies that connect to this (media tactical) history: the testament of literature in casu that of Kafka (as a machinic literature), the testament of the Autonomia movement in Italy (by focusing on the trial of many of their members held in the early eighties), the testament of computopian ideas to use new technologies to create a new participatory literature (Ted Nelson), the testament of a new arising media condition set forth by Fritz Lang with his movie 'Das Testament of Dr. Mabuse,' and the testament of Felix Guattari's ideas on post-media, desiring machines, and minoritarian media. In the dramaturgy of these investigations, six virtual personae have been staged as 'vehicles' to connect to these 'testaments': Kaspar Hauser, Dora Diamant, Max Weber, Gershom Scholem, Titorelli, and Dr. Mabuse. These six 'voices' lead the visitor/participant into a trial in which he or she is, how Kafkaesque!, the accused party! Once inside the room, there is no clear distinction between inside or outside; yet, little time is available to speak out!

'Sie werden diesen Raum lebend nicht mehr verlassen. Es bleiben Ihnen noch drei Stunden um zu sterben.... Denn der letzte Sinn des Verbrechens ist es, eine unbeschriebene Herrschaft des Verbrechens aufzurichten. Ein Zustand vollkommener Unsicherheit und Anarchie, aufgebaut auf den zerstörerischen Idealen einer Welt die zum Untergang verurteilt ist ... .' From: *Das Testament des Dr Mabuse*, Fritz Lang, 1933

FIVE TESTAMENTS, SIX VOICES

FIVE TESTAMENTS

TESTAMENT NO. 1:
Kafka's Literary Machine

Kafka's literary work is not only one of the generally accepted classical examples of literary modernism but can also be considered as a new mode of writing, as a writing or literary machine of expression that makes experiential the 'machinic' quality of subjection of modern life and death. His literary tactics set out not to demonstrate this condition in a romanesque flow, but rather as a generic Voice that deterritorializes traditional notions of authorship, authority, and text. Viewed in that sense, his work became, at least in the eyes of Deleuze and Guattari, an example of the use of the literary genre as a 'minor literature,' as a political textual machine that articulates the fundamental doubt of an explicit division of one's own place. It stems from an unauthorized place, being constantly in the act of a beginning. It outplays easy classification, symbolizations, and significations, as it is a politics of literature in action that is neither imaginary nor symbolic. His literary legacy must be seen as an assemblage of enunciations that are basically 'gestures,' as these literary acts stem from a space where the subject of the statement and the subject of enunciation can no longer be separated. This quality offers Kafka's oeuvre its 'undecidable' or 'unfinsihed' character. Kafka's testament can be seen as a departure point of a line of flight in Western culture that lays emphasis on how the machines of expression have invaded us and produced our subjectivity.

TESTAMENT NO. 2: The Trial of the Autonomia Movement (1979)

After the riots of March 1977, the odds turned for the Autonomia movement In Italy. Their alternative, ludic, and dadaist position within the traditional political specter had presented hope and change in a stifling political gridlock swarmed with corrupt politicians (left and right). But with the riots turning into an increase of the use of firearms and more fierce tactics of protest, things took a dramatic turn on March 11, 1977, in Bologna, when a member of the Lotta Continua group, Francesco Lo Russo, was killed by the police. It marked the beginning of the 'Years of Lead' (Anni di Piombo).

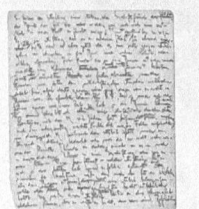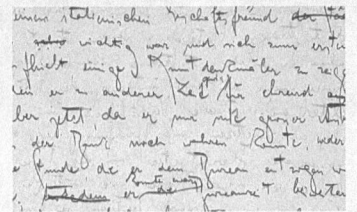

This turning to arms by the protesters was soon followed by prosecutions, trials, and incarcerations. The kidnapping and eventual killing by the Brigate Rosse of Aldo Moro in 1978 led to a monumental persecution of the far-left, as 12,000 of them were incarcerated while others fled the country. The trial (17th of April, 1979) that followed in the Aula Bunker (Foro Italico) in Rome (an old fencing school appropriated for mass trials) in which a lot of intellectuals and scholars (Toni Negri, Paolo Virno, Oreste Strano, and others) who were members of the Autonomia movement or sympathized with it, but were unrelated to the Brigate Rosse, stood trial for unspecified allegations, that in most cases were too grotesque to uphold. Nevertheless, these radical persecutions meant an enormous setback and a disentanglement of the movement. It called for different tactics, a different political approach, and new forms of activism. Amsterdam-based artist Rossella Biscotti dedicated an ongoing project on this trial and its circumference that showed on the Documenta 13 (2012). This work, 'Il Processo' ('The Trial'), incorporates a lot of the audio material that was recorded during the trials that were transcribed and translated. Part of the work is that, during sessions, these transcripts are read to an audience. Statements by Virno and Negri are amongst these transcripts.

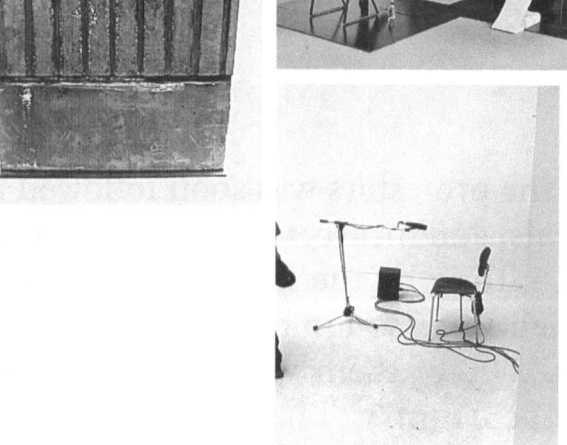

The statements, reacting to the ridiculous allegations and the extreme, severe conditions in which the prisoners were kept, resemble a Kafkaesque scene but were actually recorded at the trial. No literary imagination had to be applied.

TESTAMENT NO. 3: The Legacy of Literature and Computopianism (Literary Machines)
In his seminal work 'Hypertext 2.0, The Convergence of Contemporary

Critical Theory and Technology,' George Landow had already in the early nineties pointed to the parallelism between advances in critical theory and those in computer software design. When examining Ted Nelson's 'Literary Machines / Dream Machines' (1970), one encounters deconstructionist, or post-structuralist, notions and concepts, and, alternately, when examining the work of Derrida or Barthes, it is obvious that those writers had ideas that strongly resemble computing concepts as hypertext, networks of references, and non-sequential authoring. Conceived as a liberation from the confinements of inadequate or restricting systems of classification, and to permit the following of natural proclivities for 'selection by association, rather than by hierarchical indexing,' it was early on in its development that the expressive and literary qualities of this style in computing were recognized. This tradition thus set in computing has not only intensified the way we deal with (electronic) text but points to the fact that critical theory promises to theorize hypertext, as hypertexts promise to embody and thereby test aspects of critical theory.

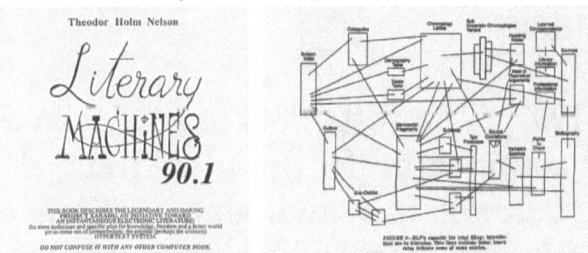

In its decades-long development, Nelson's Xanadu project has met its various versions, amendments, alterations, and expansions. Due to the enormous boost in advances in computing, the explosion of the Internet, and a radically shift in the computer and software industry; the project still seems to be a viable and critical concept for dealing with vast amounts of data, multimedia files, text, and libraries of hyperlinks and complex references. Rather an information ecology than a repository. It is this ecological media approach that forms the lens through which we look at this testament in emancipatory computing. For it points to a fundamental characteristic of hypertext: it is a topography of writing and an idea of literature as being a Borderless text; the form of text would never be fixed or static, constantly merging with new versions, adaptations, references, and cross-fertilizations. So in the context of Kafka, as put ubiquitous by Deleuze, writing is a diagrammatic action; it draws various maps on top of each other. Hypertext, then is the advance in textual graph-making, demonstrating that writing is like mapping: the superimposition of various versions as diagrams, temporal forms that resist and struggle while dealing with the unstable nature of a terrain (context) in which the act of writing is situated.

TESTAMENT NO. 4: Fritz Lang's 'Testament of Dr. Mabuse' as a Prophecy for a Ubiquitous Media Condition

Made in 1933, 'The Testament of Dr. Mabuse' is Lang's second sound film. In the film, Lang develops a film language where sound, text, and image are connected with questions of the unconscious, madness, and genius. In applying this cocktail, he deals with problems concerning the role of the subject in the era of mass media. As in most of his work, modern media are seen as an aspect of the human experience, or in some cases, vice versa. Dr. Mabuse is locked in an asylum and remains a silent film personality, yet the doctor that treats him, Dr. Baum, becomes an extension of the criminal plans concocted and written down by Mabuse. Instructed via telepathy by Mabuse to put to work these written plans, Baum's acts are accomplished through sound on a grammaphone. The relation between Mabuse and Baum, between writing and recording, between the mad man and the brilliant doctor, is a variation on the classical theme of the doppelgänger. But as pointed out by Friedrich Kittler, writing and recording become two ways of putting a function of the body elsewhere, to deconstruct the self in time and space, as both Mabuse and Baum are not present at the crimes they commit.

Radio, records, and telephone may be considered as the most apparent technologies to displace a part of the body: the recorded voice is often understood as an index rather than a symbol, a trace of the 'real' when compared to film pictures, or even more to written words. Lang uses a few spectacular ghostlike scenes where we can see Mabuse in a double exposure handing over his testament. The photographic montage, where one image is posed on another, concretizes the idea of the division of the self and the integration with another person. In one image, all the three media are put together. One media is shown after the other, the voice remains 'acousmatic.' The impression is given that Mabuse's spirit is a non-spirit, a filmic body, a screen, where separated forms of media are put together. Released in the decisive moment for the Third Reich to gain absolute power, the film was banned and discarded as being 'entartet,' (degenerate) as the Nazi's understood very well the critical warning the film made towards the potentiality of media to become a ubiquitous, inescapable condition that, as a ghostlike being, can invade consciousness in order to subject.

'La crise actuelle des médias et la ligne d'ouverture vers une ère postmédias constituent les symptômes d'une crise beaucoup plus profonde.'
Félix Guattari, from: "Pour une refondation des pratiques sociales," article in *Le Monde Diplomatique*, Oct. 1992, pp. 26—27.

TESTAMENT NO. 5: Deleuze & Guattari (D&G) Concept of a Minoritarian Literature, Desiring Machines, and a Post-Media Practice

D&G were an inspiration to the Autonomia movement in the seventies after they published their Anti-Oedipus book. In it, the idea of the Machine became a prominent feature of a new orientation to analyze subjectivation from a heavy mix of Marxism and anti Freudianism (even anti Lacanianism). It proposed the idea of a Becoming. Later on in their work on Kafka, this idea of Becoming became the model or idea for a new tactical use of media. It became the foundation of their ideas of minoritarian media. Becoming Minor. As it became an important concept during the nineties when tactical media became a force that tried to influence the development of the Internet and shape an activism that was even picked up by big corporations (Shell, for example) and state institutions. Even the Israeli army used the ideas of D&G in their tactics to fight Palestinian resistance. (see Eyal Weizman: 'Walking through walls') So, given this rather obscure insight into today's warfare, what else can we expect the legacy of D&G to bring to us? What could their testament be, after decades in which they were in the forefront of artistic debates and discourse? Yet now it seems that the pervasive nature of their presence calls for a critical analysis of their legacy, and a call for a redefinition of a tactical media practice. Maybe the white, splendid isolation of gallery spaces is not the place to remember and reiterate the glorious days of critical media use, but the place to ignite soft subversions and micro-revolutions that can enter tactically via the ear drums.

SIX VOICES

VOICE 1: *Kaspar Hauser*, a neglected orphan, who, in his communication, deregulated the form and content of each utterance. His formal interest in communication as something alien can be linked to the alienating effect of the Kafka machine.

VOICE 2: *Max Weber*, An anti-positivist sociologist and political economist who studied rationalism and modernity in its link to the belief systems and ethical values (protestant ethics and capitalism) that resulted in bureaucracy and the legal nation state in the West. His brother that was familiar with his work and was a novelist who included notions of Weber's sociology in his work. It has been proven that those texts belonged to the library of Kafka.

VOICE 3: *Dora Diamant*, the lover and inspirer of Kafka in his last years. This communist actress (agitprop), inspired by Brecht, brought Kafka two things: communism and an interest in Zionism. Kafka is said to have died in her arms. She kept a large portion of Kafka's notebooks and texts, but they were confiscated by the Gestapo. They were later found in the archives of the Stasi (DDR).

VOICE 4: *Titorelli*, a character in 'The Trial.' He inherited the title of Court Painter from his father, he knows a lot about the comings and goings of the Court's lowest level, and he offers his help to Joseph K. Because of his deep understanding of the process against K., he explains that no defendant is ever acquitted, so his tactics would be a stalling of the trial.

VOICE 5: Gershom Scholem, a scholar of Judaism and Jewish mysticism (e.g., Kabbalah). A friend of Walter Benjamin, he tried vehemently to understand

Kafka's 'jewishness' but was unable to despite all his might and even with the help of Benjamin. He wrote very poignantly about the Golem.

VOICE 6: *Dr Mabuse*, a character in a series of films by Fritz Lang. An enigmatic figure that in the film 'Das Testament des Dr. Mabuse' becomes a phantom, a ghost that has the potential to invade the minds of the people he wants to influence by telepathy. He is wicked in his interest and out for crime. He could be the forbearer of the Internet. At the end of the movie, he is only a mechanical, disembodied voice.

"I hope, that in our archives and historical filings of the future, we do not allow the techie traditions of hierarchy and false regularity to be superimposed to the teeming, fantastic disorderliness of human life."   *Ted Nelson*

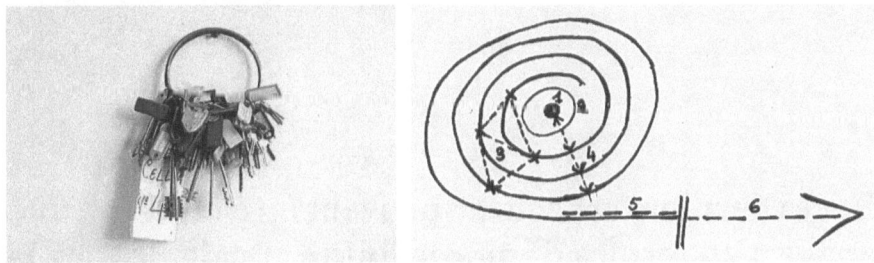

"Fritz Lang's 'Das Testament des Dr Mabuse,' in a wonderful way, rendered this spectral ghost-like dimension of the voice, realising that voice never simply belongs to the body. This is just another example of how a conservative, as if he were afraid of the new medium, has a much better grasp of its uncanny radical potentials. The same applies today. Some people simply say: 'What's the problem? Let's throw ourselves into the digital world, into the internet, or whatever....' They really miss what is going on here."   *Slavoj Zizek*

'La puissance de suggestion de la théorie de l'information a contribué à masquer l'importance des dimensions énonciatrices de la communication. Elle a souvent conduit à oublier que c'est seulement s'il est reçu qu'un message prend son sens, et non simplement parce qu'il est transmis. L'information ne peut être réduite à ses manifestations objectives; elle est, essentiellement, production de subjectivité, prise de consistance d'univers incorporels.

Et ces derniers aspects ne peuvent être réduits à une analyse en termes d'improbabilité et calculés sur la base de choix binaires. La vérité de l'information renvoie toujours à un événement existentiel chez ceux qui la reçoivent. Son registre n'est pas celui de l'exactitude des faits, mais celui de la pertinence d'un problème, de la consistance d'un univers de valeurs. La crise actuelle des médias et la ligne d'ouverture vers une ère postmédias constituent les symptômes d'une crise beaucoup plus profonde.'

Félix Guattari

'Kafka is not, as some have said, a nineteenth-century writer imprisoned in family conflicts. He is a twenty-first-century writer describing the earliest stages of a problem whose implications we are barely beginning to grasp today.'

Félix Guattari

MEMO-14

Mother says, look at people's eyes, when they speak to you. It is very rude if you don't Sometimes she asks me if I am deaf. Otherwise, the doctor should take a look at it. Once I have been to the doctor's consultation hour. He said that my shoulder was overloaded and that I should listen, very carefully to my own body, otherwise it does not heal. When my father says that I do not listen, he says that I am East 'Indisch' deaf. My best friend, next door, is also Indisch, So I got it from her. I lent her my voice recorder. So that she can listen to her own body. I hope she will recover soon. At the moment she's been doing pretty well. It almost looks like she doesn't need the voice recorder anymore. Sometimes I see her practicing in the mirror with a hairbrush in her hand. Once I told her that I had to admit that her body is very beautiful to listen to. Her body responded with a red colour. This reminds me of my Granny, who responded slowly in a grey colour. She was also deaf. I don't want to be grey. I'd like to have my voice recorder back.

MEMO-15

Hello, voice! How are you? I meet you (too) once more. Can you hear the click? I am familiar with gladness. You are stunned, to be perplexed? Pardon me. Goodbye.

MEMO-19

Félix Guattari is dead… Gilles Deleuze is dead… And I'm also not feeling that well…

MEMO-23

(the stranger) Then the judge stood up, as if to give me the signal that the examination was over. He simply asked, in the same weary tone, if I was sorry for what I had done. I thought about it for a minute and said that more than sorry, I felt kind of annoyed. I got the impression he didn't understand. But that was as far as things went that day. Apart from these annoyances, I wasn't too unhappy. Once again the main problem was killing time. Eventually, once I learned how to remember things, I wasn't born at all… I realized then that a man who had lived only one day could easily live for a hundred years in prison. He would have enough memories to keep him from being bored. In a way, it's an advantage.

BACKGROUND SPONGE PACKAGE

- replay the inner of the package (blackbox) autonomous work
- trying to eliminate my own body completely
- producing a self-generating work
- recording of bureaucracy: post, customs, art
- approaching bureaucracy (an art exhibition) with a work of bureaucracy (deconstructive work that just exists because it is traveling to the exhibition).

LETTER AND LITERATURE

(a highly influential and present act in Kafka's work (Subjektkonstitution, Autorensubjekt, das Ich...) from a lecture description: "Das mit den neuen Übertragungstechnologien zu konstatierende Ende einer "Epoche der Post" sei, so Jacques Derridas ebenso melancholische wie provozierende Folgerung, zugleich das Ende der Literatur, wie sie durch eine lange Tradition postalischer Übertragung geprägt wurde: mit spezifischen Merkmalen wie Briefgeheimnis, Adressierung, Nachträglichkeit usw. Im Rückblick also untersucht das SE, was Briefe waren: für eine medienbewusste Literatur des 18. bis 20. Jhs., aber ebenso für die Subjektkonstitution und ihre Geschlechtercodierungen, für die Bedeutung (weiblicher) Autorschaft oder für Wissens- und Machtsysteme. In ausgewählten Brief- und Posterzählungen sowie literarischen Korrespondenzen (etwa von Choderlos de Laclos, G. Keller, Th. Fontane, H. James bis hin zum Problem der Post bei F. Kafka oder I. Bachmann) sollen die Postsysteme und Medienformate als Bedingungen des Schreibens sowie andersherum die literarischen Texte zugunsten einer Erhellung der Postgeschichte gelesen werden."

KAFKA, BÜROKRATIE UND REGIME

"Jede eigentlich soziologische Untersuchung müßte die Begriffe ungemein viel feiner differenzieren, als wir es hier für unseren begrenzten Zweck tun. Gemeinschaften können ihrerseits Gemeinsamkeitsgefühle erzeugen, welche dann dauernd, auch nach dem Verschwinden der Gemeinschaft, bestehen bleiben und als 'ethnisch' empfunden werden. Insbesondere kann die politische Gemeinschaft solche Wirkungen üben. Am unmittelbarsten aber ist dies bei derjenigen Gemeinschaft der Fall,

welche Träger eines spezifischen 'Massenkulturguts' ist und das gegenseitige 'Verstehen' begründet oder erleichtert: die Gemeinschaft der Sprache."
Max Weber

DORA DIAMANT
in The Kafka Machine Epilogue quotes. Reconstructing in a text the content of a YouTube Video.
by Gosia Kaczmarek

Foucault: "For a long time ordinary individuality, everyday individuality remains under the threshold of description. To be looked at, observed, described in details, followed from day to day by uninterrupted writing was a privilege. The chronicle of the man, the account of his life, his historiography written as he lived out his life formed a part of the rituals of his power. The more one posses power of privilege, the more one is marked as individual by rituals, written accounts, visual reproductions. The name and genealogy that situates one within a kinship group, the performance of deities that demonstrates superior strength, which arc immortal in literary accounts the monuments or donations that brings survival after death, all these are procedures of an assenting individualization. In a disciplinary regime, on the other hand, individualization is dissenting. As power becomes more anonymous and more functional, those on whom it is exercised tend to be more strongly individualized. It is exercised by comparative measures that have norm as reference, rather than genealogy giving ancestors as point of reference." Video narrator: *The norm is a new reference point, and yet the thing that makes individual intelligible to discipline is in large parts a collection of attributes of his delinquencies and pathologies. For instance, only 23% of the British population has no personality pathologies.* Foucault: "For the disciplined man, no detail is unimportant. But not so much for the meaning that it conceals within it, as for the hold it provides for the power that wishes to seize it." Video narrator: *The rituals of truths are precisely what Kafka has enacted. The ordinary objects in the K.'s room can even reveal hidden truth about his case.* Foucault: "We must cease once and for all to describe the effect of power in negative terms, it excludes, it represses it censures, it abstracts, it masks, it conceals. In fact power produces. It produces domains of objects and rituals of truth. The individual and knowledge that may be gained it belongs to this production, as individual renders himself as disciplined object through questionnaires, the self-dimagnosis, the profile, interview, application or testimonial. When one wishes to individualize the healthy, normal, law obeying adult, it is always by asking him how much of a child he has in him, what secret madness lays within him, what fundamental crime he has dreamed of committing. With the development of dissenting individuality disciplinary methods, lowers the threshold of describable individuality and make of this descriptions a means of control and method of domination. And this new describability is all the more marked in disciplinary framework as a strict one. The child, the patient, the madman, the prisoner were to become with increscent ease from XIX century, the object of individual description and biographical accounts." Video narrator: *Biographical accounts, but also autobiographical once as well is an effect of disciplinary societies incitement to discourse. Joseph K. comes to feel that the only hope for his trial is to write a full and complete account of himself, for the powers that be, what the novel calls petition.*

All will be well he thinks when he has rendered himself inside out into the registries of discipline, where he will finally be fully intelligible to the power. Actor playing Joseph K. voice: "Admittedly the petition meant almost an endless task. One needed be particularly faint of heart to be easily persuaded of the impossibility of the finishing of the petition. Not because of the laziness of the decision that only kept the lawyer from finishing, but without knowing the charge and all its possible ramifications of one's entire life down to the smallest actions and events would have to be called to mind, described and examined from all possible sides." Video narrator: *The disciplinary societies cannot function without an individual articulating himself as a subject of power and its terms of intangibility. This disciplinary effect, whereby an individual articulates himself into registries of power, uses the innovative details of discipline and attributes of identity, just like Joseph K. drives himself towards the authority and its recognition. K. waited from day to day throughout the following week for further notification. He could not believe they had taken his waiver of interrogation literally.*

When the expected notification had not arrived by Saturday evening, he took it as an impressed summons to appear in the same building at the same time. So the movement of K. is not restricted, and yet that free-willed movement brings him deeper and deeper into the trial. The same is true of freedom of speech. There is no suppression of thoughts or expression in the world of "Trial." K. has no difficulty in voicing his protest. He can even rail against the authorities to their faces in a public manner possible. And yet this freedom of consciousness and expression follows a disciplinary desire, as expressed by what Joseph K. thinks of as his strategy in an opening confrontation, he wants to slip into his guards thoughts somehow and turn them to his own advantage or accustom himself to them. Foucault: "This turning lives into writings is no longer the procedure of heroization. It functions as a procedure of subjectivization and objectification. This written individualization is no longer a monument for future memory but a document for possible use. These documentary techniques make each individuality a case at which in one and the same time constitutes an object for a branch of knowledge and a hold for a branch of power." Video narrator: *So whereas at the beginning of his trial, K. had imagined that he was merely performing as a disciplined subject, he would play along with the trial. It turns out that those performative acts are precisely how the individual becomes subjected. One may object that the concept of performance suggests that the individual retains the psyche reserve independent of discipline. But look at Joseph K. He thinks he is merely performing discipline, but he believes simultaneously that the only way out of the world of discipline is to explain himself deeply and fairly, to inscribe himself evermore diligently into the tables and registries of power. Only with this act of registry is a subject created as a subject and rendered intelligible to disciplinary power.* Foucault: "The individual was constituted as the describable, analyzable object not in order to reduce him to specific features as did naturalists in relation to living beings. But in order to maintain him in his individual features under the gaze of permanent corpus of knowledge." Video narrator: *These techniques of producing the individual subjects as intelligible objects were developed in a newly systematizes penitentiary and various correctional institutions that were its cousins.*

But Foucault argues that these techniques spread outwards to hospitals, schools, and institutions that may or may not have been born of the state. Kafka's novels reflect the ubiquity of modern discipline as a mechanism that permeates the very nervous system of society in the fact that there is no distinction anywhere between private and public space and in the fact that everybody in his life, including those whom K. imagines as belonging to a strictly separate world from his private affairs, turns out to be connected somehow to the court. In its most effectively pervasive form, then, discipline is a part of the ordinary weave of life and operates without violence struggle or incarceration. In the "Trial," there is no trace of prison. Some of the most significant mechanisms of rendering the marginal subject were inspired by institutionalization of the psyche. The rendering of the mad and abnormal intelligibly to discipline created a vast system of classification, an intricate tablature of pathology. The names of pathologies created in 19th century aren't the names of realities discovered in the psyche; they are a production of discipline. I think the most interesting cultural indications of our devotion to discipline are in the way we have explained the work of Franz Kafka to ourselves.

The interpretations that exist on film of Kafka are representatives of the fact that we would rather believe him saying that the individual is free from discipline until he is threatened by violence, coercion, and imprisonment. Thus in the most exclaimed adaptation of the "Trial" directed by Orson Welles in 1963, Welles feels compelled to insert into Kafka's vision precisely the repressive hypothesis the novel clearly rejects. As the guards search through Joseph K.'s lodgings in the film, Welles has K. announcing quotation in the film. Actor playing Joseph K. says: "I'm sorry to disappoint you, but you won't find any subversive literature or pornography." Video narrator: *Welles' thesis is clear: the state is coming down on Joseph K. to repress the desire within him that is otherwise free of discipline. It is predictable from the history of individualization we have already glimpsed that Welles chooses to represent this repressed desire as sexual desire.* Actor playing Joseph K. says: [Through the lens of Kafka's *The Trial*, 1915, the work of Michel Foucault is examined Voice three: Dora Diamant, Project by Gosia Kaczmarek] "I can remember my father looking at me straight in the eye, "Come on you boy," he would say, "exactly what have you been up to?" And even if I haven't been up to anything at all, I'd still feel guilty. You know that feeling, when the teacher at school making an announcement that something is missing from her desk, "All right listen everyone…" that was me of course, I'd feel sick with guilt, and I did not even know what was missing… Maybe, yeah… that must be it unless your thoughts are innocent, one hundred percent…can that be said of anybody? Even saints have temptations…" Actor playing K. leans down to kiss actress lying next to him. Video narrator: *The worst offender, however, in the raising of Kafka's vision of disciplinary society and replacing it with Orwell's totalitarianism, is surely Steven Soderbergh's ridiculous film "Kafka." Soderbergh depicts the world of kidnapping, torture, and imprisonment. A regime of body snatching, as the protagonist puts it. The film loudly reiterates one of the most common glaring misinterpretations of Kafka's work by portraying it in every frame as a paranoid vision. It is rare to find commentary on Kafka's novels that does not rely on a concept of paranoia. Soderbergh obligates this misreading by posing in his film a hidden, removed, and coordinated totalitarian power easily embodied in the figure of a single despotic mastermind. In the "Trial," however, the paranoid vision is the mythology that the novel exploits. One of the reasons that most adaptations have failed to capture both the nightmare and the comedy of Kafka's works is that they did not want to acknowledge that K.'s trial is an organism without center and one that has already enlisted the subject himself. There is no man behind the curtain; the inaccessibly high judges about whom K. hears so much in the novel are merely legends. There is no coherent inaccessible center of power that is keeping its eye on Joseph K. It seems that our collective imagination wants to replace Kafka's depiction of permeating discipline with a comforting depiction of monstrous Orwellian totalitarianism. Comforting because we can always say with relief that we are not there yet.*

DORA'S "CARIER" PAGE NINE OF HER KAFKA DIARY

"It is time to say at this point, that when I get to it, i.e., when I have time to do it, my notes on Franz will be better than they have been up till now.

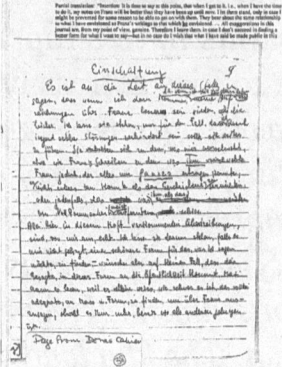

I let them stand, only in case I might be prevented for some reason to be able to get on with them. They bear about the same relationship to what I have envisioned as Franz's writings to that he envisioned... All exaggerations in this journal are from my point of view, genuine. Therefore I leave them, in case I don't succeed in finding a better form for what I want to say—But in no case do I wish that I have said be made public in this..." http://www.youtube.com/watch?v=UmfH2KOTx4g&feature=B-Fa&list=PL8E410D87ADDBB177&index=28

CHAPTER 1

POEM/ SLOGANS: Analysis, Self-self-criticism, Analysis, Self-criticism, Analysis, Self-self-criticism, Analysis, Self-criticism, Analysis, Self-self-criticism, Analysis, Self-criticism, And do you get a right wing orgasm? Do you like our slogan 'Fuck the System'? Destroy what destroys you!

An email from the WEB: You are receiving this mail in regards of the freemason confraternity of the whole wide world (FCWWW). You are moving well in what you are doing but in order to make it easier for you, we have concluded for you to be a part of us as a member to sign your life to us and have anything you Need. Be it anything in the whole wide world. You can't refuse us now for it's too late. Get back to us now for your Illuminati membership Order and also for you to know more about the ancient ILLUMINATI FORUM and also the Orientation and goals that we pursue. Get back to acquire your goal now.

CHAPTER 5 (HISTORICAL DOCUMENTS)
excerpt

ULRIKE MEINHOF QUOTE:
read on the street en passant

"It is pointless to explain the right thing to the wrong people. We've done enough of that. We don't want to explain our actions to babbling intellectuals, to those who are freaked out, who know it all anyway, but rather to the potentially revolutionary section of the people. That is to say, to those who can immediately understand our actions, because they are themselves prisoners. Those who want nothing to do with the blather of the "left," because it remains without meaning or consequence. To Those who are fed up!"

AUDIO SAMPLES:

audio sample—Ulrike Meinhof (interview) audio sample—Klaus Kinski (speech) audio sample—Ton Steine Scherben—Macht kaputt was euch kaputt macht (song) mixed W/ audio sample—Louis Armstrong—Mack the Knife (song) audio sample—Eugen Georg/Gluklya Pershina Utopian Clothes street demonstration Amsterdam audio sample—Eugen Georg—boogie-down zizek (mashup Zizek/Krs-One) Audio sample—Don Backy : canzone (song) Voice four: Titorelli, Project by Eugen Georg. Voice five: Gershom Scholem, Project by Jefta Hoed

248

16. *Scholem an Benjamin. {Jerusalem,]* 17. 7. 1934
(s. Briefwechsel, 157/J

Die *Unvollziehbarkeit* des Geoffenbarten ist der Punkt, an dem aufs Allergenaueste eine *richtig* verstandene Theologie (wie ich sie mir, in meine Kabbala versunken, denke und Du ihren Ausdruck ja gerade in jenem offenen Brief gegen Schoeps fs. Briefwechsel, S. 27, Anm. 2], den Du kennst, einigermaßen verantwortlich gegeben finden kannst) und das was den Schlüssel zu Kafkas Welt gibt, ineinanderfallen. Nicht, lieber Walter, ihre *Abwesenheit* in einer präanimistischen Welt, ihre *Unvollziehbarkeit* ist ihr Problem. Hierüber werden wir uns zu verständigen haben. Nicht so sehr Schüler, denen die Schrift abbanden gekommen ist — obwohl auch das schon keine sehr Bachofensche Welt ist, in der das passieren kann! - als Schüler, die sie nicht enträtseln können, sind jene Studenten, von denen Du am Ende sprichst [s.o., S. 37]. Und daß eine Welt, in der die Dinge so unheimlich konkret und jeder Schritt so unvollziehbar wird, einen *verworfenen* Anblick und keineswegs einen idyllischen bieten wird (was Du unverständlicherweise für einen Einwand gegen die »theologische« Deutung zu halten scheinst, da Du erstaunt fragst, seit wann ein Gericht der höhern »Ordnung« je so sich präsentiert habe wie das auf den Dachböden tagende), das freilich scheint mir überaus zwingend. Andererseits hast Du natürlich in sehr weitem Maß recht in Deiner Analyse der Gestalten, die in solcher Weise sich allein behaupten können; ich bin durchaus nicht bereit, das zu bestreiten, es ist etwas von der »hetärischen« Schicht darin und Du hast das ganz unglaublich meisterhaft herausgeholt. Einiges habe ich nicht verstanden - was Du von K raft zitierst, schon gar nicht, Aber ich hoffe vielleicht auf einzelnes in dem Essay, wenn Du mir das Manuskript läßt, noch einzugehen, speziell auch was das »Jüdische« hier angeht, das Du mit Haas in Ecken suchst, wo es doch in dem Hauptpunkt so sichtbar und ohne Umschweife sich erhebt, daß man Dein Schweigen darüber als rätselhaft empfindet: in der Terminologie des Gesetzes, die Du so hartnäckig nur von *ihrer profansten* Seite aus zu betrachten Dich versteifst. Und dazu war kein Haas nötig! Die *moralische Welt der Halacha* und deren Abgründe und Dialektik lagen Dir dort doch unmittelbar vor Augen [seil, in Kafkas »Prozeß«], Ich schließe heute, weil dies abgehen soll.

26. *Benjamin an Scholem. Paris, 12. 6. 1938*
(1. Teil; s. Briefwechsel, 266-273)

Kafka lebt in einer *komplementären* Welt. (Darin ist er genau mit Klee verwandt, dessen Werk in der Malerei ebenso wesenhaft *vereinzelt* dasteht wie das von Kafka in der Literatur.) Kafka gewahrte das Komplement, ohne das zu gewahren, was ihn umgab. Sagt man, er gewahrte das Kommende, ohne das zu gewahren, was heute ist, so gewahrt er es doch wesentlich als der *Einzelne* von ihm betroffene. Seinen Gebärden des Schreckens kommt der herrliche *Spielraum* zu gute, den die Katastrophe nicht kennen wird. Seiner Erfahrung lag aber die Überlieferung, an die sich Kafka hingab, allein zugrunde; keinerlei Weitblick, auch keine »Sehergabe«. Kafka lauschte der Tradition, und wer angestrengt lauscht, der sieht nicht.

DISAPPEARANCE [TAG : BAUDRIL-DISAP-PEARANCE]

"Art in itself in the modern period exists only on the basis of its disappearance-not just the art of making the real disappear and supplanting it with another scene, but the art of abolishing itself in the course of its practice. It was by doing this that it constituted an event that it was of a decisive importance. I say 'was' advisedly, for art today, though it has disappeared, doesn't know it has disappeared and—this is the worst of it—continues on its trajectory in a vegetative state. And, thus becomes the paradigm of everything that survives its own disappearance."

Source: 'Why hasn't Everything Already Disappeared?', Jean Baudrillard, 2007

SLEEP [TAG: SLEEP]

'Sleep, sleep, sleep, go to sleep sleep go to sleep

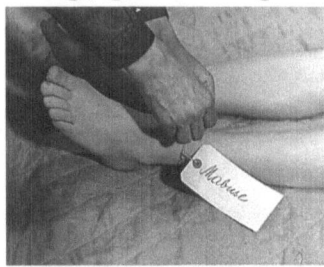 

you are now in a deep sleep in store promises endless possibilities a life of ease a life cocooned in a routine of food stimulus and response softness is a thing called comfort doesn't cost much to keep in touch we never forget you have a choice possibilities in store a taste of paradise success on a plate for you endless promises sleep, sleep, sleep, go to sleep you are now in a deep sleep' .   *Source* : 'Sleep', *This Heat*, 1980, from the album 'Deceit' Voice six: Dr. Mabuse, Project by Willem van Weelden

THE KAFKA MACHINE: A THREE HOURS TESTAMENT
A Project on Autonomia, Abstract Machines, Voices, & the Production of Subjectivity

a project by DOGtime IDUM Gerrit Rietveld Academie, Amsterdam
Jelmer Luyting, Alexander Schierl, Gosia Kaczmarek, Eugen Georg, Jefta
Hoed Willem van Weelden, 2012

Commissioned by HEAD WORK.MASTER, LAPTOPRADIO, As part of the
project : La Radio Siamo Noi, Extended Nervous Systems and White Rabbits
26.04-26.05.2012 LiveInYourHead, Geneva

The Kafka Machine consisted of: An Apple Mac Mini running an Isadora
patch, and a non-functional microphone

Three sections were programmed: The Sage, The Merchant, The Warrior
The 6 voices (Kaspar Hauser, Max Weber, Dora Diamant, Titorelli, Gershom
Scholem, Dr Mabuse) were distributed in these three conflicting areas.

Editorial supervision: Willem van Weelden Design poster and flyer: Alexander
Schierl Technical support: Jamie Griffiths, Rombout Willems Software :
Isadora, Troikatonix Inc., Mark Coniglio Big Thank You to: Laurent, Ceel,
Jamie, Rombout, Manel!

OCEANICS   Yann Chateigné

In French, the term "radio" has two meanings, depending on the pronoun that one places before it. *La* radio (feminine) defines the concept of radio itself, the ensemble of channels that compose its programs, or the device that is used to tune in. *Le* radio (masculine) is the person who, at sea, on a ship, is in charge of radio communications. This double analogy can be applied the same way to the very notion of wave itself. One qualifies by wave any form of oscillation through matter, which means in the meantime the radio waves, electromagnetic frequencies, carry out sounds in the air at the speed of light and the masses of water that are put in motion by elements through the liquid immensities of the seas.   A novel from 1954 by Greek poet, sailor, and radio officer Nikkos Kavvadias, *The Shift*, folds these two dimensions over each other. The book recounts the life aboard a ship full of men who consider their life a curse, living like prisoners in a traveling cell in which radio transmissions represent the only connections with the outside world. Out there, the role of the radio is one of a receiving apparatus: *le* and *la* radio merge together to become an abstract machine, channeling the voices, sounds, and calls of the living men. Noise, rumors, and fluxes of the elements melt with words, information, and memory, all transformed by the radio officer character and his device, into poetry, turning the travel inwards.   *Oceanics* offers a ninety-minute-long voyage through four decades of modern composition, electronic music, and sound art. It draws "an ocean in between the waves" from electromagnetic experimentations using brain-waves by Pierre Henry and Alvin Lucier, who turn composition into an abstract travel through mental pulsation, to the recent technological sound spaces by *Oneohtrix Point Never*. Historical New Age composers such as Jürgen Müller or Suzanne Ciani make the listener dive into oceanic feelings, while the dark and emotional atmospheres created by Sylvia Monnier, something like forty years later, mirror a more claustrophobic world.

Cosmic metaphors cross multiple open sonic paths, from beginning to the end: the electro-acoustic compositions by Bernard Parmegiani drive us underwater, to the "aquatopic" universe of techno unit Drexciya, while conceptual ambient music by The KLF lights the way to the planets of the Solar System, which movements influence on the tides of the oceans. Progressively, the trip opens up to a series of images of the sea itself, interweaving visions of digital oceans (Emeralds), flows and floods (Lambkin & Lescalleet), crepuscular timelessness (Sunn O))) & Ulver). Poet and occultist Aleister Crowley concludes with a poem from 1920 entitled *At Sea*, talking about the dissolution of the self in the dark waters of the unknown, finally making this tape entering the immensity of nothingness.

List Selected by Yann Chateigné:
— Pierre Henry, Voyage—Mise en musique du Corticalart de Roger Lafosse (1971)
— Bernard Parmegiani, Aquarythm—Chants magnétiques (1974)
— Alvin Lucier, Music for Alpha Waves, Assorted Percussion, and Automated Coded Relays, composed in 1980

- Imaginary Landscapes: New Electronic Music (1989)
- Jürgen Müller, Dream Sequence for a Jellyfish—Science of the Sea (1982)
- Suzanne Ciani, The Fifth Wave: Water Lullaby—Seven Waves (1988)
- The KLF, Neptune—Space (1990)
- Drexciya, Wave Jumper—The Quest (1997)
- Emeralds, Alive In The Sea Of Information—What Happened (2010)
- Oneohtrix Point Never, Stress Waves—Returnal (2010)
- Sylvia Monnier, Skin Waves—Never More Camellias (2012)
- Graham Lambkin & Jason Lescalleet, Kingdom 3 (Submerge)—Photographs (2013) Sunn O))) & Ulver, Eternal Return—Terrestrials (2014)
- Richard Skelton, Of the Sea—Verse of Birds (2012)
- Aleister Crowley, At Sea, recorded circa 1920—from The Great Beast Speaks (1999)
- Stephen P. McGreevy, Eastern Nevada Growler Whistlers—Electric Enigma: The VLF Recordings Of Stephen P. McGreevy (1996).

Delphine Bedel (FRA) is a photographer, publisher and researcher, specialised in emerging publishing practices. www.delphinebedel.com

Franco "Bifo" Berardi (ITA) is one of the founders of the famous *Radio Alice* in Bologna and an important figure of the Italian *Autonomia* Movement. He is a writer, media theorist, and media activist.

Francesco Bernardelli (ITA) is an art writer, curator and lecturer working in the interzone of contemporary art, time-based media and performance. www.francesco-bernardelli.blogspot.ch

Donatella Bernardi (CHE) is a multidisciplinary artist working with installations, publications, films, essays and exhibition curatorship. She is currently in charge of the MA Fine Arts program at ZHdK. www.donatellabernardi.ch

Yann Chateigné (FRA) is a critic and curator. He has served as chair of the department of visual arts at the Haute école d'art et de design in Geneva from 2009 to 2017.

Alfredo Cramerotti (ITA) is Director of Mostyn, Wales, and an Editor. He co-curated Manifesta 8 as CPS Chamber of Public Secrets and co-directs AGM Culture, roaming curatorial agency.

Nadia EL-Imam (SWE) is an engineer and designer. She is founding director of *Edgeryders*, a company living in symbiosis with an online community of about 3000 hackers, activists, radical thinkers and doers, and just normal people that want to make a difference. www.edgeryders.eu/en/company/home

Jonathan Frigeri (CHE) is a sound artist and an electronic musician. Founding director of Zonoff a non-profit organisation that promotes different art languages through radio, publications and events.

Kenneth Goldsmith (USA) is a poet. He is the founding editor of UbuWeb, teaches Poetics and Poetic Practice at the University of Pennsylvania, and is a Senior Editor of *PennSound*. He hosted a weekly radio show at *WFMU* from 1995 until June 2010.

Felix Kubin (DE) is an electronic musician. He regularly collaborates on theatrical and animation productions, writes radio plays and is a self-described dadaist.

Lars Bang Larsen (DNK) is an art historian, curator, and writer. He is now adjunct curator at Moderna Museet, and guest professor at the Royal Art Academy, both in Stockholm. In his PhD he investigated relationships among art, psychedelia, connectivity, and cybernetics in the 1960s and 1970s, and their resonances in contemporary art.

Quinn Latimer (USA) is a poet and critic, whose first book, *Rumored Animals*, won the 2010 American Poetry Journal Book Prize. Latimer was documenta 14's editor-in-chief of publications.

Andrea Marioni (CHE) is an artist, journalist and adventurer.

Federica Martini (ITA/CHE) is an art historian, curator and MA Program Coordinator at ECAV. She is the curator of the *Museum of Post Digital Cultures*, founded with Elise Lammer in 2013. www.postdigitalcultures.ch

Ceel Mogami de Haas (NL) is an artist and curator. He is founding director of the artist-run space *One Gee In Fog* located in Geneva.

Jealousy Party (IT) is a Berlin based abstract R&B outfit blending noise and improvisation with funk, avant rock, dub and idiosyncratic electronic collage—a fusion they term *Punca*.

Ergo Phizmiz (UK) is a writer, composer, collagist, theatre & opera maker, radio producer, songwriter, and performer.

Angelo Plessas (ITA/GRC) is an artist whose practice investigates the changing role of art and social relations in the time of internet. www.angeloplessas.com

Robin Rimbaud aka Scanner (UK) is an artist and composer working in London, whose works traverse the experimental terrain between sound, space, image and form.

Laurent Schmid (CHE) is an artist, publisher and teacher at *Work.Master*, HEAD-Geneva. He won't give up searching and trying out concepts and models which may permit liberating subjectivity. http://electric-haze.net/

Joël Vacheron (CHE) is a journalist and sociologist writing mainly about music, photography and design.

Willem van Weelden (NLD) has a background in social philosophy and visual art. He has published on new media in various magazines and catalogues. He was involved in numerous new media projects as a creative director and coach. Currently his focus is on writing and teaching (i.a. Gerrit Rietveld Academie).

Giovanna Zapperi (ITA) is an art historian and critic. She received her doctorate from the École des hautes études en sciences sociales (EHESS) in Paris in 2005. Her work examines the interrelation of art criticism, visual culture and feminism.

ON RADIO AND AUDIO ART

ARNHEIM, Rudolf. Radio Aesthetics. Manchester, NH: Ayer Co Pub, 1971 (original in english, London 1936)

AUGAITIS, Daina, LANDER, Dan. Radio rethink. Banff: Banff Center Press, 1994

BRECHT, Bertold, Der Rundfunk als Kommunikationsapparat. Rede über die Funktion des Rundfunks; Vorschläge für den Intendanten des Rundfunks; Radio—eine vorsintflutliche Erfindung? All in: BRECHT Bertolt, Werke, Bd. 21, Schriften I, Berlin: Aufbau Verlag. 1988.

CEBREROS URZAIZ, Carmen, Gallet, Bastien Labelle Brandon, eds. Radio Memory (Audio Issues). Berlin: Errant Bodies Press, 2008

DANIELS, Dieter, Kunst als Sendung, Von der Telegrafie zum Internet. München: Beck, 2002

DIEDRICHSEN, Dietrich, RUHM Constanze (eds.). Immediacy and Non-Simultaneity: Utopia of Sounds. Publications of the University of Fine Arts Vienna: Vienna, 2010

FISHER, Margareth. Ezra Pound's Radio Operas, The BBC Experiments, 1931—1933. Cambridge: MIT Press 2002.

GILFILLAN, Daniel. Pieces of Sound. German Experimental Radio. Minneapolis: University of Minnesota Press, 2009.

GRUNDMANN, Heidi ed./ Zimmermann Elisabeth et al. ReInventing Radio. Aspects of Radio as Art. Frankfurt a. Main: Revolver, 2008.

JOSEPH-HUNTER, Galen. Transmission Arts: Artists And Airwaves. New York: PAJ Publications, 2011.

KAHN, Douglas. Noise Water Meat, A history of sound in the arts. Cambridge: MIT Press 2001.

KAHN, Douglas, Whitehead, Gegory. Wireless Imagination: Sound, Radio, and the Avant-Garde. Cambridge: MIT Press, 1994

LABELLE, Brandon. Acoustic territories : sound culture and everyday life. New York, London: The Continuum International Publishing Group, 2010

LABELLE, Brandon, Granly Jensen, Erik. Radio Territories. Los Angeles / Copenhagen: Errant Bodies Press, 2007

LABELLE, Brandon. Radio Memory (Audio Issues). Los Angeles / Copenhagen: Errant Bodies Press, 2008

MANDL, PLATENGA, STRAUSS, David, Bart, Neil (Eds.), Radiotext(e), New York: Semiotext(e), 1993

MILLER Paul, D. (aka DJ Spooky That subliminal kid). Rhythm Science. Cambridge, Amsterdam: Mediawork / The MIT Press, 2004

ROSSET, Christian, Yann Paranthoën, L'art de la radio, Arles: Phonurgia, 2009

SILBERMAN, Marc. Brecht on Film and Radio, Bertolt Brecht. London: Methuen Pub Ltd, 2000

STUHLMANN, Andreas (Ed.) Radio-Kultur und Hör-Kunst. Zwischen Avantgarde und Popularkultur 1923-2001. Würzburg: Königshausen u. Neumann, 2001

THURMANN-JAJES, Anne ed./ BREITSAMETER Anne / PAULEIT, Winfried. Sound Art, Zwischen Avantgarde und Popkultur, Schriftenreihe für Künstlerpublikationen. Bremen: Salon, 2005.

STRAUSS, Neill, MANDL, (Ed.), Radiotext(e), Neill Strauss. New York: Autonomedia Press, 1993

WEISS, S. Allen. Experimental sound and radio. Cambridge: The MIT Press, 2001

WEISS, S. Allen. Phantasmic Radio, Durham. London: Duke University Press Books, 1995

COLLETTIVO A/TRAVERSO, ed. Alice è il diavolo. Storia di una radio sovversiva, Milano: ShaKe Edizioni, 2007

COLLECTIF A/TRAVERSO, ed. Radio Alice, radio libre, Paris: Laboratoire de Sociologie de la connaissance, 1977

A SHORT LIST ON AUTONOMIA, POST-MEDIA, F. GUATTARI

BERARDI, Franco. Thought, Friendship, and Visionary Cartography. New York: Palgrave Macmillan, 2008

BRADLEY, Bill, HANNULA, Mika, RICUPERO, Cristina and SUPERFLEX. Self-organisation / Counter-economic Strategies. Berlin, New York: Sternberg Press, 2006

DEULEUZE, Gilles, GUATTARi, Félix. Kafka: Toward a Minor Literature, Minneapolis: U of Minnesota Press, 1986

GENOSKO, Gary. Felix Guattari: An Aberrant Introduction. London: Continuum International Publishing Group, 2002

GENOSKO, Gary, ed. The Guattari Reader.
Oxford: Blackwell Publishers, 1996

GUATTARI, Félix, NEGRI, Antonio. New
Lines of Alliance: New Spaces of Liberty.
London/New York: Autonomedia, 2010

LOTRINGER, Sylvère, MARAZZI, Christian.
Italy: Autonomia, Post-political politics. New
York: Semiotext(e), 1980

VIRNO, Paolo, HARDT, Michael, eds. Radical
thought in Italy: a potential politics.
Minneapolis: U of Minnesota Press, 1996

A big thank you to all who generously helped us
and to all who were part of the LapTopRadio
group. Active members of the group were over
the time:

Constance Allen, Sophie Alphonso, Leila
Amacker, Laeticia Bech, Sacha Beraud, Sarah
Burger, Ashley Cook, Stephane Devidal,
Johanna Di Dio, Camille Dumond, Fabien
Duperrex, Aaron Fabian, Sabrina Fernandez,
Vianney Fivel, Ravi Govender, Kevin
Gotkovsky, Romain Grateau, Pauline Guiffard,
Nelly Haliti, Romain Hamard, Hugo Hemmi,
Anne Hildbrand, Yu Weng Julia Hung, Jungung
Jang, Charlotte Khouri, Galaxia Roijade
Konungur, Mara Krastina, Quentin Lannes,
Nina Langensand, Renaud Loda, Renaud
Marchand, Andrea Marioni, Lou Masduraud,
Sébastien Mennet, Coline Mir, Arttu Palmio,
Camilla Paolino, Sébastien Press, Liliane
Puthod, Lena Quelvennec, Elena Radice, Teemu
Rasanen, Beau Rhee, Simon Riat, Pekka Ruuska,
Emma Souharce, Ramaya Tegegne, Anne Le
Troter, Roman Urodovskikh, Léonie Vanay,
Camille Vanoye, Emeline Vitte, Martina-Sofie
Wildberger, Seda Yildiz, Salomé Ziehli

LapTopRadio: La radio siamo noi

Publisher: Link Editions
Editors: Laurent Schmid with Ceel Mogami de Haas and Jonathan Frigeri
Graphic Design: B&R, Noah Bonsma and Dimitri Reist, Bern

Authors: Delphine Bedel, Francesco Bernardelli, Donatella Bernardi, Yann Chateigné, Alfredo Cramerotti, Nadia EL-Imam, Kenneth Goldsmith, Lars Bang Larsen, Quinn Latimer, Andrea Marioni with Franco Bifo Berardi, Federica Martini, Angelo Plessas, Laurent Schmid, Joël Vacheron with Tex Royale and Alexis Milne, Willem van Weelden, Giovanna Zapperi.

Exhibition "La Radio Siamo Noi" at LiveInYourHead, Geneva: curated by Mathieu Copeland, Ceel Mogami de Haas, Jonathan Frigeri, and Laurent Schmid.

Talks and Inputs (*La Radio Siamo Noi*, *Wonderlust*, *Sanatorium* and other projects linked to Work.Master, HEAD — Genève): Fabrizio Basso and Francesco Bernardelli, Federico Campagna and Richard John Jones, Francesco Cavaliere & Leila Hassan, Mathieu Copeland, Paolo Coteni, Alfredo Cramerotti, Vincent Chanal de Rouguin, Fucking Good Art—Rob Hamelijnck and Nienke Terpsma, Kenneth Goldsmith, Goodiepal—Kristian Vester, Samuel Gross, Morten Norbye Halvorsen, Raimundas Malasauskas and Marcos Lutyens, Quinn Latimer, Federica Martini, Antonio Monroy, Jonas Ohlsson, Bohdan Stehlik and Una Szeemann, Joël Vacheron, Willem van Weelden, Robert Whilite.

Vinyl and Cassette: Jonathan Frigeri. Contributions by: Delmore fx, Goodiepal, Johnny Haway, Felix Kubin, Ergo Phizmiz, Jealousy Party, Scanner

Translation: Megan J. Bredeson (Giovanna Zapperi), Gora Nicoletti

Transcription: Andrea Marioni, Ceel Mogami de Haas

Copy editing: Katharine Turvey, Ceel Mogami de Haas, PRS, Gora Nicoletti, Laurent Schmid

Proofreading: Katharine Turvey, Scribendi Inc., PRS proof reading service

Mastering vinyl: Paul Jones

The publication is supported by the strategic fonds of HES-SO

ISBN: 978-0-244-40622-6

www.ingramcontent.com/pod-product-compliance
Lightning Source LLC
Chambersburg PA
CBHW061343280526
45784CB00001B/117